A SILVER-PLATED SPOON

A
SILVER-PLATED
SPOON

by

JOHN, DUKE OF BEDFORD

THE REPRINT SOCIETY LTD : LONDON

FIRST PUBLISHED 1959
THIS EDITION PUBLISHED BY THE REPRINT SOCIETY LTD
BY ARRANGEMENT WITH CASSELL & COMPANY LTD 1960

PRINTED IN ENGLAND BY
HAZELL WATSON AND VINEY LTD AYLESBURY

ACKNOWLEDGEMENT

I should like to thank Miss Gladys Scott Thomson, of Somerville College, Oxford, who has written many books about the early history of my family, and knows much more about it than I do. She has very kindly allowed me to draw on many of the facts she has culled so painstakingly from outside sources.

BEDFORD

Woburn Abbey
April, 1959

CONTENTS

ILLUSTRATIONS IN PHOTOGRAVURE
(between pages 112 *and* 113)

The eleventh duke, my grandfather
Mary, wife of the eleventh duke—my grandmother
The twelfth duke, my father
The State Dining-Room
The Library
The Canaletto Room
The Saloon

CHAPTER ONE

THE INDISCREET PARLOUR-MAID

LIVE like a duke—the phrase has become part of the English language, conjuring up visions of yachts, country mansions, retinues of servants and the fat life in general. People still seem to equate it with the idea of being born with a silver spoon in one's mouth, never lacking in creature comforts, having no worries and, in this modern age, no responsibilities—a happy round of coronets, grouse moors and champagne.

I often wonder whether the hundreds of thousands of people who visit Woburn Abbey every year think this is the sort of life I have led. They see this lovely house the Russells have owned for over four hundred years and assume, quite reasonably, that it has always formed part of my existence. Yet I was well into my teens before I even saw it or knew that the Duke of Bedford was the head of my family. I was kept away from school and other children and then more or less abandoned in a Bloomsbury students' hostel with ninety-eight pounds a year while my parents' marriage broke up. My father disinherited me when I chose to marry the woman I loved. I worked as an estate agent, a journalist and in an export firm until I exiled myself to South Africa as a fruit farmer, when there seemed no hope of coming to terms with my father.

Then he was found shot. I became the head of a family whose estate was threatened with extinction. Now I am engaged in a desperate struggle to maintain our ancestral home intact with its priceless art treasures, although it does not belong to me and I have no final say in what is done with it.

My grandfather and father did their best to see that I

would have no part in the administration of the Bedford estates, but I find myself almost the last obstacle to its disappearance as a family possession. It is all a very odd story.

Woburn is one of the loveliest of England's stately homes. It stands as a monument to the architectural genius of Inigo Jones and Henry Holland. Its treasures include Canalettos, Van Dycks, Holbeins and the Armada portrait of Queen Elizabeth, all relics of the part the Russells have played in the history of England. It gives more people pleasure than any building of its kind in the whole country. The lakes where my ancestors used to shoot ducks in moody solitude are now thronged by happy children in little paddle boats. The eleven and a half miles of wall which my forbears built to keep their neighbours at bay now serves to protect herds of rare animals in their natural surroundings for the delight of our innumerable guests. From the dusty suburbs of London and the Midlands thousands of people find an oasis of green which helps them to return to their week's work refreshed. Our visitors come from all over the world. By making them welcome we try and share the happiness we enjoy in possessing such a unique establishment.

I first saw Woburn under very different circumstances. It must have been about 1933, when I was sixteen. The extraordinary thing is that until that time I had no idea that I was the potential heir to the Bedford title. Heaven knows, my family has acquired something of a reputation for eccentricity over the generations, but nevertheless people may find this situation hard to believe. It will give some idea of the extraordinary circumstances in which I was brought up.

I had never been to school. My father had been sent to Eton and had hated it. So I suppose he had made up his curious mind to shelter me from the unseemly outside world. Instead of having some common sense knocked into me as a boy, life did not start administering its kicks until I was nearly grown up, a painful experience I am determined none of my sons shall share. Mine was a world of nurses and tutors, bereft of parental affection, and with no stimulus to learn anything, not even the facts concerning my family background. I knew of course that my father was the Marquess of Tavistock and that I, as his elder son, carried the title of Lord Howland. It simply never occurred to me that my grandfather was a duke and as there was a complete conspiracy of silence on the subject, there was no reason why it should.

My father was a perfervid pacifist all his life. It was the earliest of his many cranky notions and had led to a complete split between him and his father before the First World War. For twenty years thereafter they had neither seen nor spoken to each other and never communicated. I first found out who I was from one of my father's parlour-maids.

At the turn of the nineteen-twenties and -thirties the newspapers carried frequent accounts of the exploits of the 'Flying Duchess' of Bedford. She had become quite a figure, qualifying as a pilot when well into her sixties and taking part in a number of record-breaking flights. The most famous were a round trip to India and another to the Cape, but she was always getting involved in some forced landing, in being attacked by eagles, or shot at on the wing by Moroccan tribesmen, and the press always had some new story to tell. Quite how the subject came up I cannot remember, but I shall never forget my incredulous surprise when this little maid said: 'But that is your grandmother.'

It is quite clear that the servants knew all the circumstances. I can only suppose they had been sworn to silence while I was growing up. The fact that a new parlour-maid knew more about my family than I did gives some idea of the general atmosphere. At that particular time it was rendered even more chaotic, as my parents' marriage was in process of breaking up and I was about to be farmed out for another period in my spasmodic education to the house near Cambridge of Canon Raven, who was a friend of my father's. As far as I recall my father was up in Scotland at the time, and I wrote asking whether all this was true and if so whether I could write to my grandparents. After some considerable delay, during which he got in touch with them through other members of the family, I received permission to do so—such was the protocol of relationships—and in due course I received a summons to present myself at Woburn.

This must all sound quite impossible, like something out of one of those incredibly artificial Victorian novels. I had no idea what to expect when I arrived at what is, after all, my ancestral home. All I remember now is that I travelled by slow train from Cambridge across country, and when I got out at Woburn Sands station there seemed to be no one to meet me. All the other passengers dispersed, their cars and traps drove away, and I was left to my own devices. I thought I had better try to get a taxi, but there was none available. It was only then that I looked again at a great big, high, old Rolls-Royce on the other side of the road, with an elderly lady in the driver's seat, who seemed to be watching me. I walked over and asked very politely whether she could tell me where I could get a taxi to Woburn. 'Are you Ian?' she asked rather sharply and I said I was. It was my grandmother. I was to discover that another of her hobbies was bird watching, and I suppose she regarded me as another specimen of some sort. She had been keeping me under observation for five or ten minutes, presumably to make up her mind what sort of person this long-lost grandson was.

After that beginning, conversation was not easy. To add to my difficulties in making a good first impression, she was stone deaf, which made her a terrifying driver. She drove very fast, was quite incapable of hearing whether anything else was coming or not, and we rocketed along the country lanes as if we had a couple of highwaymen on our tails. We arrived far too early for lunch, so she took me for a long drive round the park. It was all quite lovely, and some-how not part of this world at all. Three thousand acres and more, with eleven and a half miles of brick wall all round it, with my grandfather's rare herds of bison, Père David deer and Highland cattle, roaming freely across the meadows or dodging back into the woods and copses. We drove past the hangar where my grandmother kept her 'planes and, although she only made some cursory remark about her flights, the feeling of restraint started to lessen. Then we came to the house.

It was larger then than it is now, in a hollow square instead of U-shaped. It still had its east wing, together with the big riding-school and indoor tennis-court which ran between the two stable blocks. But it was not a happy or welcoming house. There was an awful sombre chill about it —not the least reason why I try to make it a more cheerful place these days. I would hate to have my guests repeat my first experience.

My grandmother handed me over to relays of about half a dozen footmen, who led me through what seemed miles of corridors to a little room with a wash-basin and a brass can in it, where I was temporarily abandoned. I washed my hands, waited, peered out of the door, could see nobody and was finally rescued after what seemed an interminable wait by an elderly lady named Miss Flora Greene who had been my father's governess, and had stayed on to become a sort of housekeeper-companion and general go-between to shield my grandfather from the outside world. She was extremely grand, had been governess to the German Kaiser's family at the turn of the century, and is the only person not a Russell to be buried amongst my ancestors in the family mausoleum in the parish church of Chenies in Buckinghamshire. She led me through another maze of corridors, full of pictures and display cabinets, to a room full of Canalettos where, after an interlude of stilted conversation, my grandfather appeared.

Square, bulky, medium height, grey-haired, he was gruff and formal. I had arrived all eager to make an impression on this formidable forbear, but the attempt fell flat from the start. He had a curious habit of always looking down when he talked and a disconcerting way of deadening every conversational gambit. It was either 'Indeed', or 'Quite', or just silence, rather like playing tennis and having the other person hitting the ball into the net the whole time.

There was no grace of manner, no welcome, no attempt to exert any charm at all to the young fellow who, in all likelihood, would one day bear his title. The subject of my father never came up and he clearly was not very interested in me. It was the most formal and deadening interview I had ever experienced, the forerunner of many such. After a few minutes silence fell and we went into lunch.

This was a grim and monosyllabic affair. We sat in an enormous room surrounded by half a dozen flunkeys, and the whole thing was over in about twenty minutes. There was no flow of conversation, just a few short remarks and answers, with everybody deferring to my grandfather. My grandmother tried to interest him in a wild duck or goose which was nesting somewhere in the park, but after a few desultory exchanges the subject collapsed. I knew nothing about geese so I steered clear of the conversation. Neither of them seemed to know how to cope with me at all and I had the feeling that I was a distinct embarrassment at the table. Any attempt to introduce small talk would have been like blowing a bugle in the British Museum, so I thought discretion was the better part of valour and kept mum.

The food, what you had time to notice before the course was whisked away, was very good in a simple fashion, but I noticed that my grandfather had the very odd habit of having a cube of ice put in his glass of what I thought was uncommonly good claret. As he lifted it I noticed what beautiful hands he had, the well-kept hands of someone who had never had to do a stroke of work in his life. After the meal we went and sat briefly in the *salon*, my grandfather in the only comfortable chair and the rest of us on a set of hard-padded leather sofas with cretonne covers. After a short tour of the house with Miss Greene I was packed off to the station again, this time with a chauffeur. My father's name had never been mentioned once. The subject was clearly taboo.

Over the years that followed I became a vague appendage of this self-centred household. I doubt if I was there more than two or three times a year, sometimes staying a couple of nights, but usually just for the day. My grandfather lived an extraordinary life. He had an income of well over two hundred thousand pounds a year and lived completely isolated from his contemporaries and the affairs of his times. His only concern was the administration of his estates. He regarded himself as something of an innovator in agriculture and forestry, and wrote one or two books on the subject which I believe are classic examples of how not to run such matters. He regarded it as modern and up-to-date to sell off landed property and buy stocks and shares because the return was greater. Unfortunately he picked such equities as Russian bonds and completely overlooked the possibilities of capital appreciation on land. Otherwise Woburn was run exactly as it had been since the eighteenth century. Even the means of getting there from London belonged to the stage-coach era. He maintained two large houses in Belgrave Square, both kept fully staffed, although I doubt if he was in them twice a year, usually to attend the meetings of the Zoological Society, of which he was the president.

He kept four cars and, I think, eight chauffeurs in town, eating their heads off. They were responsible for the first part of the journey down to the country of any guests. The town car used to take you as far as Hendon, where you had to get out and join the car which had been sent up from Woburn. You never travelled with your suitcase, that was not considered the thing to do. It had to come in another car, so you had a chauffeur and a footman with yourself, and a chauffeur and a footman with the suitcase, with another four to meet you. Eight people involved in moving one person from London to Woburn. This régime went right on until my grandfather died in 1940.

Sometimes, as an alternative, the oldest car, with the oldest chauffeur, would pick you up and deposit you at Euston, where he handed you a first-class ticket. At the other end, another great barouche would be waiting to take you to the house. There you were allotted your own personal footman, who stood behind your chair at meals, while a small army of another fifty or sixty indoor servants kept

17

the archaic household going. My grandfather had refused to install central heating at Woburn except for the corridors, so that there were always seventy or eighty wood fires crackling throughout the Abbey in the winter, even in the bathrooms. Each bath was a great tank with mahogany edges and there were always piles of warmed towels. It was comfortable enough in an impersonal sort of way, but you were almost frightened to move around the house in case you got in my grandfather's way.

There were still a number of oil lamps around and one man had the sole duty of trimming them and keeping them filled. They had tried to install electricity once in the early years of the century, but a section of the wiring had caught fire and they returned to primitive methods until not very long before I went there for the first time. Twenty-odd years later, when I was living in the house with my own family, I had to have much of the old wiring re-done. It seemed to have been installed in a very slap dash fashion and I asked the estate electrician why it had been done so badly. He explained that my grandfather had never allowed any workmen to be seen in his presence, and when they were putting the wiring up the main staircase they had to post two men, one at the top and one at the bottom, to keep watch. If my grandfather appeared in the distance they all ducked into a cupboard until he had gone past.

Even so the new system of illumination baffled some of his contemporaries. One old friend came down the next morning to complain rather querulously that the lighting in his room was very bad, with only one candle. There was indeed a candle, but it was left there for guests to seal letters with wax. It had escaped this old gentleman that there was an alternative system of lighting available, so orders were given for large black and white enamel plaques to be made and installed above the switches with the words *Electric Light*.

The housemaids all had to be five feet ten inches tall or over. They were more or less bought to measure. When the guests went upstairs at night they were handed a candle and a silver tray, on which was a glass of milk and a biscuit and a basket of fruit. I suppose everyone was afraid that the electricity might break down again, but it made an awful conglomeration of things to stagger up the stairs with.

If you wanted to smoke, you were led off to a grim little room on the ground floor, behind four or five sets of doors, to have your cigarette. It was rather as if you were taking a shot of cocaine or hashish. Miss Greene would ask in hushed and conspiratorial tones if one wished to smoke, as if it was very daring and modern to suggest such a thing at all. The guest was then ushered off, while everyone studiously pretended not to notice. The smoking-room is now my secretary's office and to this day seems like a den of iniquity with an aura of evil-doing still clinging to it. The Duke of Windsor told me that he was the only man who had ever smoked in my grandfather's presence. However, as you left the house at the end of your stay, a footman stood by the front door carrying a tray laden with all kinds of cigars and cigarettes, from which guests were invited to take their choice, presumably to smoke in the car or train.

In the midst of all this magnificence my grandfather lived a completely lonely and austere life. He had no contemporaries or friends of his own and most of the people who came to stay were cousins or other relatives. He had very little time for human beings and rarely spoke. My grandmother, being deaf, used to say that as he never started a conversation and she never heard anything, there was no sense in anybody coming to the place. Hardly anybody ever did.

Most of the time was spent in waiting around, and everything went by the clock. Everyone went into breakfast together, and we all had to be ready and assembled by the time he appeared, so that we could sweep in behind him. Breakfast was at eight-thirty, lunch at one-thirty and dinner at eight, on the dot. He had picked up the habits of an aide-de-camp in his early army days and attended to every detail of the administration of the house himself. Every car that left the Abbey had to have a chit signed for it, authorizing it to leave the garage. Even if my grandmother wanted to take a car out, she had to have a chit signed by him in person, directing the garage to release a particular car for the purpose. He had a fixation about not being diddled or swindled and of course he was diddled and swindled right, left and centre, as such people always are.

The food was simple but always extremely good. I found my first visit was no exception to the general rule. No meal lasted more than half an hour, usually considerably less. At his end of the table my grandfather had a large mahogany three-tiered dumb-waiter, with plates of radishes, spring onions and other appetizers that he would pick from. No one else was offered any, they were just there for him. His first course was always a cup of beef *consommé*. It was made exactly the same way every day, using precisely nine and a half pounds of best shin of beef, and one kitchen-maid only was entrusted with the making of it. Even when she married she was brought back into the house for the purpose. On his birthday he varied his claret with ice to the extent of drinking champagne, half a bottle of which was served to him alone. Beer never made its appearance at table, although it was brewed in one of the outhouses for the purpose of washing the oak floors, to bring out the colour and polish the wood. The old housekeeper told me in later years that when they scrubbed the floors afterwards the fumes used to make them quite tipsy. One unfortunate footman who was caught one day drinking the beer out of the bucket instead of spreading it on the floor was sacked on the spot.

Both my father and grandfather were the least clothes-conscious men I have ever known. I was allowed to go round with clothes that were either bulging with tucks to be grown into, or with my arms and legs sticking out of a suit that was too old and too small. Their clothes were made in the fashion my grandfather had worn as a young man, grey-green for the country, silk hat, morning coat and striped trousers for London, although my father wore a blue serge in town. I cannot remember either of them ever buying a new suit in my lifetime. My grandfather had

20

never been in a shop and never carried any money in his pockets. His country suits were a high-cut jacket with knickerbockers fastened below the knee with elastic. He never used a wardrobe. In one of the four dressing-rooms opening off his bedroom at Woburn he had four long, plain, wooden trestle tables. His sixty or seventy suits were folded across them like clothing at a jumble sale.

He slept in an old brass-knobbed bed with a bumpy mattress. One day its condition got so bad that the housekeeper thought she would have it remade. She had it replaced, but was brought up late in the evening and very nearly got the sack. The old one had to be fetched back again, with all its lumps and holes, and he kept it to the end. Its valley and hills just fitted him and he would not have it changed.

Miss Greene was the power behind the throne. She had set up my grandfather on a pinnacle and even relations wrote to her first before communicating with him. He never spoke on a telephone and it was practically impossible for anyone to get to speak with him at all, except heads of departments on the estate, and they were all terrified of him. He took tremendous trouble over Woburn and the other estates, improving the shooting and amenities. To this extent he was very hard-working, but entirely self-centred and selfish. He did all this administration work extremely well, but without any emotion. He had a high sense of duty and responsibility, had served in the Guards, been an aide-de-camp out in India, a member of the Bedfordshire County Council and Mayor of Holborn, but, when I first met him, lived in a complete backwater.

He did his duty as a duke, was a member of various societies although, apart from the Zoological Society, he hardly ever put in an appearance, gave large donations to charity and had been made a Knight of the Garter. He had held no major public appointment, although I believe at one time he was offered the Governor-Generalship of Canada. He simply was not interested in that kind of thing. He took no part in social life and was not ambitious in any way. He

21

had everything that money could buy and that was enough for him.

Pride of family I suppose he had. He thought it was his job to continue in the traditions of the past. Older members of the family would tell me he was very distressed that his son did not share these interests, and I think he felt very strongly that things would never be the same again. I have no reason to suppose that he was particularly pleased with me either, but then I have never suffered such boredom as in his company. He never said anything that was interesting. I cannot remember him uttering a single noteworthy sentence. He had tremendous knowledge on some subjects. If someone talked about animals or trees he could probably give the answer to a question, but it was done in a manner completely and utterly dead, like an encyclopædia.

He did not even display overt pride in the lovely things in Woburn. He was interested in them in so far as they were part of the tradition, part of the background of the place, but he had no feeling for them, no affection. He carried this considerable sum of knowledge in his head but made no attempt to impart it. On one or two occasions I walked round the house with him in complete silence. If I asked for information, it was provided in the shortest possible number of words, although occasionally there was a dry note of humour to some of his comments. At least they seemed amusing, because anything that broke the tension was welcome.

The only tangible expression of his interest was the collection of rare animals whose descendants live to this day in Woburn Park. It was he who really built up the herds of bison and Père David deer. Apart from that, he had no literary or intellectual pursuits of any sort. He wrote the shortest letters I have ever known, usually about twenty words, the exact expression of his own personality, completely flat and uninteresting. He used to buy masses of very dreary contemporary biographies. There are whole shelves still full of them. Paintings or objects of vertu simply did not interest him. If they had some connexion with the family in the past or had belonged to some previous duke, he might buy them for their historical association, but never for pleasure. He had no taste in furniture and bought nothing but ugly pieces from fashionable modern furnishers. My grandmother was no better. She had some of the superb Louis XIV and Louis XV chairs they had inherited well scrubbed and painted white, which is the condition they are in to this day—a terrible piece of vandalism.

He had been the ground landlord of the whole Covent Garden estate in his time, part of the manorial lands we had inherited from our ancestors. However he had disposed of the Covent Garden properties before the First World War for something like two million pounds, most of which had been invested, very unwisely, in Russian bonds, of which my trustees still have a useless crateful somewhere. He had retained the private Bedford boxes at the Drury Lane Theatre and Covent Garden Opera House, which our forbears had insisted, as of right, in having built into them, but I doubt if he ever attended a single performance.

They both had private entrances leading from the street, and the boxes were never sold to the public. Special passes were issued by his estate office, a few of which came rather grudgingly my way over the years. We had to ring a special bell and the door was opened by a scarlet-coated, powdered footman in the Bedford livery. I must have been the only member of my family for three generations with an ear for music. There were at least twenty pianos down at Woburn, but nobody played them. I doubt very much whether they were even kept in tune. One of them was encrusted with mother-of-pearl, but it might just as well have been boxed in a crate.

*   *   *   *

Harmony was, I fear, a quality conspicuously lacking from the lives of both previous generations of my family. My father's marital problems attained more public notoriety, but my grandfather and grandmother lived isolated lives of their own, at least by the time I met them, and this had been true for many years. They had met when he was still Lord Herbrand Russell, younger son of the ninth Duke of Bedford. His elder brother was heir to the title, apparently in good health, and my grandfather, one of the many Russells who never went to school, but was brought up by governesses and tutors, had followed the familiar path of many younger sons and entered the army. In 1886 he was in India as an aide-de-camp to the Viceroy, the Marquess of Dufferin and Ava. The only human anecdote I have ever culled concerning the first twenty-seven years of my grandfather's life was that in the Grenadier Guards he apparently enjoyed the twin nicknames of 'Hatband' and 'Rousseau', which I can only surmise derived from his Christian and surnames.

It was against the Kiplingesque background of Simla that he met my grandmother. Her maiden name was Mary Du Caurroy Tribe, and she was the daughter of the Archdeacon of Lahore. I do not suppose the competition was very great, but she was considered one of the local beauties. The sparse records of the time also make her out to have been something of a bluestocking. She had been educated at Cheltenham Ladies' College and the first sign of what was to develop into a lifetime interest came when she attended secretly a series of Red Cross lectures. For this scandalous departure from the norms of behaviour expected of a young lady she was taken away from the school and brought back to India. There, until she met my grandfather, she compounded her frustrations by retiring at frequent intervals to the top of the steeple in her father's church, where she learnt Indian dialects and made friends with a bat. One of the military heroes of the time, Lord William Beresford, V.C., who was military secretary to the Viceroy, persuaded her to come down from the belfry long enough to attend a viceregal ball, where she was introduced to her future husband. They were married at a place with the almost fictional name of Barrackpore at the beginning of 1888 and then returned to England.

From all accounts she had a pretty frigid welcome. My

24

family have always thought themselves slightly grander than God and energetic steps had been taken to try to stop the marriage. These had proved unsuccessful, so two of my great-aunts were sent, I think to Marseilles, to make sure that my grandmother wore the right clothes and looked respectable before she could be accepted into her new environment. They cannot have sent back a very favourable report as I have heard it said that her mother-in-law walked straight out of the house and never came back again. Be that as it may, the newly married couple soon retired to Scotland for the grouse-shooting season and took the lease of an estate called Cairnsmoor in Galloway, which was to remain their Scottish home for the rest of their lives.

It was here that my father was born, and I cannot help feeling that the circumstances of his arrival had a direct influence on the personal relationships we all later had to suffer. My grandfather and grandmother were walking together alone across the moors one bitter winter morning, only four days before the Christmas of 1888, when she suddenly realized that her child was about to be born. With an icy wind whistling round them and the cries of wild birds as their only company, they had to seek shelter in a derelict shepherd's cottage, the only building in sight. There was no doctor, no midwife, only a couple of hurriedly summoned farm servants. My father was born on a rough couch of heather, something which our hardy ancestors of Tudor days might have survived better, but which was certainly a cause of lasting shock and distress to my grandmother. She never had another child and I very much doubt whether she and my grandfather ever lived together again as man and wife. He had always wanted a large family and for the rest of his life remained a withdrawn and disappointed man.

His father died in 1891 and two years later his elder brother also died, unexpectedly, without issue. He had become the eleventh Duke of Bedford, together with all the other titles of which I shall have to tell the story, Marquess of Tavistock, Earl of Bedford, Baron Russell of Chenies,

25

Baron Russell of Thornhaugh and Baron Howland of Streatham.

The *ménage* they took over at Woburn was even more splendid than the one I came to know some forty years later. Then each guest really did have a footman behind his chair at lunch or dinner, in a livery of dark-rose coats and white breeches with powdered hair. As a final touch, each guest at breakfast had before him or her a separate little tea-pot made of gold. Even this magnificence did not prevent the owners from developing their separate interests. My grandfather had been made a member of the Zoological Society in 1872 at the age of fourteen, and although his duchess became a Fellow in 1892, it was he who took the lead in stocking the park with rare animals.

The European bison were obtained for him by his cousin, Sir Odo Russell, who was secretary at the British Embassy in St. Petersburg. They were a present from the Tsar, who was given two American bison in return. The Père David deer, originally five in number, came from various zoological societies on the Continent, where they have since died out, and the herd of wild Prejevalsky horses was bred from a group of five stallions and seven mares captured in Mongolia and the Desert of Gobi about 1900. Otherwise he devoted his time entirely to the administration of his estates. All his life he remained in spirit the aide-de-camp who had helped to administer the viceregal household in India at the time he married. The running of the house was taken entirely out of my grandmother's hands. She was told she did not know about such things, so she developed no interest in the house and had nothing to do with it at all. My grandfather even drew up the lunch and dinner menus, although in the course of time some of this work devolved on Miss Greene.

Some outdoor interests Grandmother Mary and Grandfather Herbrand did share. By sheer application she became a remarkable shot. She was the first woman to ask her London tailor to make her a ride-astride habit, and in the early pioneering days motored without a chauffeur, carrying out her own running repairs, including the changing of tyres. She also became an enthusiastic skater and a member of the Prince's Skating Club in Knightsbridge. Just after the turn of the century, when the owner proposed to sell the rink, the duchess persuaded her husband to buy up the remaining eleven years of the lease, thus prolonging the life of the club until the outbreak of war and allowing her to go skating alone whenever she wanted to. My grandfather clearly pandered to her whims, as the cheque involved was well up in the five figures.

The skating period also coincided with renewed interest in nursing. By 1898 she had opened a small cottage hospital at Woburn and herself took a course of lectures at London Hospital. She qualified as a nurse and operations sister and, in due course, as a radiologist and radiographer. The establishment was gradually expanded over the years and became a model of its kind. It must have cost my grandfather a fortune.

It was also during the Edwardian era that she developed her interest in ornithology, of which I felt myself so much the victim at our first meeting. Setting off in the ducal yacht *Sapphire*, she used to spend days on end marooned on Fair Isle for the spring and autumn migrations. In fact it was she who founded the bird-watching station there. She also ventured as far north in the yacht as Iceland and Jan Mayen Island, dragging my unfortunate father along. He was desperately seasick the whole time and when he grew up, never went out of England again, except for one notorious occasion during the Second World War.

Somewhere on this northern trip, my grandmother was presented with a small fir tree, which was brought back and put into the greenhouse at Endsleigh, the Bedford estate in the West Country. It prospered vigorously, to such a point that they soon had to put another storey on the greenhouse. Every five years or so they had to put up another extension, so that in the end the greenhouse had a tower like a pagoda. They finally had to do what they should have done in the first place, lop off the top of the tree as it grew.

My grandfather, in the meantime, was becoming involved, involuntarily, in the sort of political controversy which I am sure frightened him out of public life for good. Although he was the sort of High Tory that only a man with landed Whig traditions can become, he was by no means totally illiberal in his opinions. In 1910 he was expressing himself in the House of Lords in terms which seem to me to make uncommon sense. He said that he was against the hereditary principle as the sole criterion of membership of the House of Lords, and wanted people appointed to it from outside to make it an effective second chamber. He was also advocating that the land of England should be in more hands than it was at the time. He had given effect to his convictions by selling the freehold of parts of his property to tenants ever since he had come into possession of it. That was all right as far as it went, but he clearly had an eighteenth-century fear of the working classes. In 1912, with the war scare looming ever larger, he was expressing the opinion that if the British Expeditionary Force was fully engaged abroad there might simultaneously be a rebellion at home. The 'large, alien, hostile population in London', he thought, would without question choose this moment to rise in revolt.

He was under continuous fire in the press and Parliament as an exploiting landowner. He was accused by a Baron de Forest of imposing a tax on food by taking ground rents from his Covent Garden estate, probably not the least reason why he decided to get rid of them. In what reads to-day like an ill-advised gesture of defence, he allowed his solicitors to publish information about the village of Ridgmount in Bedfordshire, where it was claimed, apparently to his credit, that the total gross rental was three hundred and eighty-three pounds and the outgoings two hundred and seventeen pounds. Twenty-two of the occupiers were in his employment. They had one half-holiday a week on which they were paid full wages, as well as six whole holidays each year. The highest wage was twenty-eight shillings a week, earned by one of them, and the lowest, for five and a half days' work, fifteen shillings, earned by eight of them. No wonder he was able to afford something like two hundred and fifty servants on his estate.

With the outbreak of war, my grandmother converted the riding-school and tennis court at Woburn into a war hospital with eighty beds. The conflict which, among other things, was to doom their way of life, found them both at their best. My grandmother often put in sixteen hours a day at the hospital and my grandfather established, with the approval of the War Office, a training depot for the Bedfordshire Regiment on his near-by estate of Ampthill. Apart from the soldiers' food, clothing and pay, he met all the expenses himself. When the camp was turned into a command depot half-way through the war, he still made himself responsible for the welfare amenities. More than eleven thousand men passed through it to the front.

The end of the war found him firmly set in the anonymous, retiring way of life which I noticed during my first visit. I think he knew he was a survivor from another world and wanted only to live out his time. During the twenties he was still nominally active as chairman of such bodies as the Imperial Cancer Research Fund and the Bedfordshire County Council, although he retired from that in 1928 at the age of seventy, after serving continuously for thirty-two years. The Zoological Society remained almost his only outside interest, and its hundredth anniversary in 1929 found him telling the only funny story I have ever heard credited to him. His agent, he said, had once written to him: 'I beg to inform Your Lordship that the emus have laid an egg. In Your Lordship's absence I have obtained the biggest goose I could find to sit on it.'

My grandparents seldom saw each other during the day. Grandmother would come back from her work at the hospital and take grandfather out for half an hour's walk in the park in the evening. This was the one period they spent together. After dinner she would do a crossword or read the illustrated papers. My grandfather would stay for about ten minutes and then disappear into his study. They did have a certain amount of mutual respect for one another. I think my grandmother was grateful for the wealth and the life he provided and they shared an interest in animals and birds, but there was no emotion between them at all. Only once do I remember her showing concern. My grandfather had tripped during their evening walk and she had saved him from falling down. The period before dinner was spent with her solicitous enquiries as to whether he had hurt himself.

As she grew older, my grandmother developed another interest, the one by which she is best known to posterity. In 1926 she took her first aeroplane flight from Croydon to Woburn. She was by now very deaf indeed, suffering from constant buzzing in the ears, but she found that the air trip and the change in atmospheric pressure brought her miraculous relief. She was afraid that her inability to hear what was going on would deprive her of all usefulness at the hospital, and her new enthusiasm for flying came just in time to prevent a severe attack of depression. Although her association with a number of pioneering flights brought her new renown and her final sobriquet of the 'Flying Duchess', the plain fact is that her main reason for spending these long periods in the air was to stop the buzzing in her ears. Her achievements were not for that less noteworthy.

For a couple of years she flew only as a passenger in a hired D.H. Moth, principally with Captain C. D. Barnard, who was her associate in all the later record-breaking flights. In 1928, at the age of sixty-two, she started taking flying lessons from him herself. By now Barnard had fired her with his ambition to set records for various long-distance flights. She hired a big Fokker monoplane called *The Princess Xenia*, which the previous year had only just failed to cross the Atlantic, and with it they set off for India. The attempt nearly ended in disaster as they tore through a cluster of telephone wires as they took off. However they got as far as Bushire in Persia, where they had to make a forced landing with bad engine trouble, and only reached

Karachi after a six weeks' delay. The duchess returned by sea.

They tried again the following year, by which time she had bought the 'plane and renamed it *The Spider*. This time they did the return journey in eight days, a real landmark in the history of aviation. My grandmother got most of the credit although, on their arrival at Croydon, she made it perfectly clear what her part in the enterprise had been: 'I did not find it at all tiring,' she said. 'Of course it was a terrible strain for Captain Barnard, the pilot, but most of the time I sat comfortably in my armchair in the cabin and admired the scenery through the windows. I spent some time in the cockpit and handled the controls for a short period.'

Nevertheless, her enthusiasm was genuine. She had a hangar and runway laid out at Woburn and another private airfield constructed at a country house my grandfather had bought for her, called Wispers, near Midhurst. It was purchased as a dower house and as it was comparatively small he had built on a staff wing practically as large as the house itself. He could not visualize anyone living without an enormous retinue of servants. My grandmother had simpler tastes and hated the whole idea. I am sure she had determined in her own mind never to live there and indeed she never did.

Her next flight was more adventurous and she played a greater part. This was in April 1930 when they flew to the Cape and back in seventeen days. They had installed extra petrol tanks, and one of her duties consisted of pumping petrol into the wing tanks, which took her fifteen minutes in every hour of hard work in very cramped quarters. On the flight back they came very near disaster when flames from the exhaust burnt a hole in a heater pipe, allowing carbon-monoxide fumes to escape into the cockpit. My grandmother became unconscious and Barnard only just landed the 'plane in time. A violent thunderstorm caused another forced landing in the Sudan, where they had to tramp a mile through lion-infested jungle after dark to the

31

native hut where they were obliged to spend the night. My good grandmother sailed through all these trials with complete equanimity and this time really deserved some of the acclaim she received on their arrival at Croydon. It was a remarkable exploit for a woman of sixty-four.

By 1933 she was an accomplished pilot and had already done a hundred hours of solo flying, which is where, as you might say, I came in.

CHAPTER TWO

PARROTS AND PLAIN LIVING

IT took me years to piece together these fragmentary records of my grandparents' earlier life. I learnt nothing about it from my own father and for all he told me his own youth might never have existed. Family history was simply never a subject of conversation as I grew up and such details as I have of my father's early years come mainly from an autobiography that was published shortly before he died. It is a disconcerting document, full of the crankish theories and opinions which made him such a byword to his contemporaries. Not the least distressing aspect of it is that in the course of over three hundred pages he does not mention my mother or myself once. We do not even figure in the index, although there is a single reference to his father-in-law and an anecdote concerning my younger brother at the age of two. I hope this story is not starting to sound like one long complaint, but surely there is a moral to be drawn from the pointless and introspective lives my parents and grandparents lived. The sheer delight I get out of contact with people must in some way be a reaction to all the unhappy circumstances I am describing.

The Victorians and Edwardians have much to answer for. They organized themselves out of all contact with their children in a manner which I do not believe to be true of their Georgian forbears, and certainly would be regarded with aversion by all normal people nowadays. My father was a very odd character indeed, which is hardly surprising considering the frigid, formal atmosphere in which he was reared. About the only thing we have in common is that he broke with his father at the age of twenty-six and I broke with him when I was twenty-two.

Of his early life he wrote that it was bad luck both for his parents and for himself that he was a sensitive and nervous child, unable to acquire skill in many of the pursuits in which they would have liked him to excel. His father, like many of his generation, felt very strongly that no boy could be properly educated unless his training conformed strictly to that which was customary for his class. Although normally kindly and even-tempered, his father resented intensely anything which seemed to him to be unreasonable opposition and the punishment meted out was often out of all proportion to the offence.

There were occasional agreeable interludes—certainly more than I ever experienced in my turn—when he used to go and see his father every morning as he was dressing and again in the evening before dinner. On winter evenings his father would even read to him in front of the fire in the study, while the boy cooked chestnuts or Indian corn on a shovel. His mother was much less easy. Her rather hasty temper and impatience with any form of incompetence, coupled with the fact that she sometimes punished him severely for things he did not even know were wrong, made him afraid of her.

Hastings, as my father had been christened, certainly got the worst of both educational worlds. As an only child he was brought up quite alone without any other children to play with, his existence controlled by the formidable Miss Greene, who turned the nursery wing into a replica of the German Court from which she had come. My grandmother felt very little interest in him and, in any case, had his upbringing taken entirely out of her hands. When I met her in later years she told me that during her flight to Africa she had met a man who had been a tutor to my father in the house for six months, and they had never met and never spoken. Then my grandfather had him sent to school. He went to two private day schools in London and then, surprisingly enough, to Eton, all three of which he detested cordially. 'At all I was extremely miserable,' he was to write later, 'partly by reason of the unwelcome attentions of

34

bullies, partly because I was no good at school games and disliked them, partly because all my hobbies and interests were connected with home and were non-transferable.' Sodomy, he complained, was extremely common. Eton boys were supposed to have good manners, but this my father dismissed with the comment: 'Whatever their behaviour during the holidays, their conduct during the term was reminiscent of the African tribe of whom the traveller said "manners they have none and their customs are very beastly".'

He left Eton after two years with no regrets and a fine legacy of nightmares, which recurred at decreasingly frequent intervals almost up to the end of his life. He spent the last afternoon of one holiday trying to delay his return by spraining his ankle jumping down a sunken fence with tied feet and by drinking stagnant water in order to make himself ill. On one occasion he got up a tree and told his father that if he sent him back to Eton he would throw himself on the ground and kill himself. He had taken quite a stock of food up the tree with him and was clearly prepared to withstand a considerable siege. His father fingered his moustache and promised that he would not be sent back, but as soon as he had shinned down, he was firmly grasped by the ear and packed off to school. This doubtless gave my father a very limited faith in human nature.

He seems to have started very early in life to keep large collections of insects, spiders and frogs, with various tame owls and birds. As I got to know grandmother better, she often used to tell me what a difficult child my father had been. Once, in the hope of arousing his interest in the various aspects of British life, she had driven him all the way from Woburn to Scotland by car. Instead of looking at the countryside, he spent the whole time studying the behaviour of flies on the windscreen and could not be made to look at the view at all.

He kept boxes full of insects and butterflies all the time he was at school. It can hardly have added to his popularity. He then went up for four years to Balliol College, Oxford, where he added religion to his taste for bugs, and ended up with a fourth in history. That was in 1911 and brought the relationship with his parents to a climax.

In a move which must have contributed to his later pacifist views, he yielded to his father's wishes and joined a territorial regiment, the 10th Middlesex, and was attached for several months to the second battalion of the Grenadier Guards stationed at Farnborough. This he described as an intensely bitter and unpleasant experience. The conversation of the officers seemed to be limited entirely to army shop and the topics of polo and women. He hated the drill and was always getting it wrong. This period brought two or three clashes with his father and a growing feeling that his parents considered him 'a disappointing son and a vague foreboding of some more serious crisis ahead'. After attaining the exalted rank of first lieutenant, he ended his army career by resigning his commission.

The next step was his marriage, about which I have hardly any information at all. One of the professors at Oxford and an enthusiastic supporter of the Y.M.C.A. was a Mr. Robert Whitwell. His daughter, Louisa Crommelin, became my mother. How my father ever brought himself to propose I cannot imagine. By all accounts he was very shy, very cold, very reserved, with practically no friends, and full of the odd mixture of ethics, religion and principles which was to remain his mark throughout his life.

My mother once told me that she used to pray that he would propose to her sister rather than herself, but her mother, who was a terrible old snob and was enchanted with the idea of becoming connected with the dukedom of Bedford, pushed her into the marriage. I do not think that my mother ever went to Woburn. She was taken down for inspection by the family at Endsleigh and it was not long after they were married that my father and grandfather had their final quarrel. Fortunately, by this time my father had had fifteen thousand pounds a year settled on him.

With the war clouds looming, the duke wanted my father

to rejoin his regiment. What happened then had better be told in his own words, as it is all I know:

Apart from a purely personal aversion to re-entering what was to me the slavery of army life, two other feelings began to take shape with increasing clearness in my at first tortured mind. The first was that, quite apart from anything to do with selfish personal inclination, it would be definitely wrong for me, after my known and proved incapacity to do the right thing in a sudden emergency, to take a commission and then, by some blunder on the battlefield, perhaps sacrifice the lives of my men uselessly and needlessly. The second was that in this great time of crisis I ought to go and find some way—exactly what I did not know—of serving my fellow men in no matter how humble a capacity. Leaving a letter to my father behind me, telling him my reasons for feeling unable to carry out his wishes, and knowing that serious trouble lay ahead, I left home. . . . My father—understandably no doubt in view of his traditions and outlook—took my decision very badly indeed. He wrote to me that he never wished to see me again and intended to take steps to disinherit me.

The fifteen thousand pounds a year he managed to keep. The trust had been too well drawn up to be broken. But the two men did not see each other again for twenty years. At Miss Greene's suggestion my father did pay a last visit to Woburn to see his mother—while the duke was away—but that only made things worse: 'During a brief and painful interview I learnt for the first time and with a considerable shock that her views were agnostic,' is all my father finds to say. So that was that.

After the break, my father and mother spent most of the war washing dishes in a Y.M.C.A. canteen in the Victoria Barracks, Portsmouth. My father had donated the hut himself, but the work seemed to give him for the first time the sort of equilibrium he had been seeking, and in after years he used to talk about it as the happiest time of his life. It was here that he met one of the few friends I remember being associated with him, the Reverend Gordon Arrowsmith, who later became Rector of Chelsea and is still one of my trustees. Most of his other acquaintances at the time seem to have been a weird collection of pacifists and religious crack-pots. My parents had taken a house in Havant, although when I was born in May 1917, they were staying temporarily at a house in Prince's Gate in London belonging to my Great-aunt Ela.

By the time I was old enough to remember anything the war was over and my father had become embroiled with the work of the various voluntary societies which took up most of his time. He was an active member of the Prisoners' Aid Society, a sponsor of the Student Christian Movement and a committee member of something called the Conference on Christian Politics, Economics and Citizenship, where I think he first met Professor, later Canon, Raven, who became Master of Christ's College, Cambridge, and played a brief part in the curious plan of education my father devised for me.

I remember the Havant house as being a dreadful Victorian pile. It was always freezing cold, except for the aviaries full of valuable birds, which had a tremendously complicated and expensive central-heating system. On winter days I used to creep out amongst the parrots to keep warm and many a time used to steal the special imported fruits and nuts laid out for them because household sweets were so few and far between. All we normally had in the house were mouldy old apples out of the orchard. It was an extraordinary *ménage*. My father had given my mother an allowance of three thousand pounds a year when they were first married for the housekeeping and household bills. When the war broke out she returned half of it to him to help with their donations to the Y.M.C.A. and the other charitable organizations in which they were interested, but when the war ended she never saw it back again. For the rest of their marriage she had one thousand, five hundred pounds a year with which to pay the wages of about eight servants, dress herself and the children and pay all the household bills, which meant that my father had thirteen thousand, five hundred pounds to struggle along with.

I can remember my clothes were always bought much too big, with huge tucks, and then one wore them until one's arms were shooting out of every coat and one's trousers were way up one's legs. My mother never had any decent clothes at all. I can remember it being quite an event when she bought a new dress or coat. Otherwise they used to be made up at home from material she bought. The maid who did this cannot have been very good at her job, because I never remember any of them having any kind of shape or style.

I was brought up by a nanny and merely presented to my parents from time to time for inspection. Her name was Miss Parsons, but my younger sister, brother and I all called her Didi. She was the only person I ever remember showing me any warmth or affection during my early childhood. Certainly my father was incapable of doing so. I don't think all his life he really knew what it was to give affection to anybody, although he demanded it from others. It was very pathetic. We formed no part of his life at all. He used to receive thousands of letters, getting up at six-thirty in the morning to go and look at his birds and then sitting down to answer his huge correspondence. He wrote endless letters to people and to the newspapers, always in long-hand, and he was usually away somewhere either lecturing, or speaking, or doing good works. Apart from the few people connected with his charitable and religious enterprises, my parents literally knew no one and sought no one out. They had no contact whatsoever with their social contemporaries.

Another of my father's queer notions was to try out new sources of food. He knew a great deal about edible fungi and would gather revolting looking toadstools and puff balls, eat them with relish and watch his occasional guests and ourselves wrestling with them unwillingly. He experimented with the velvet from the horns of deer, which they brush off on trees at certain times of the year, and tried to

39

make dishes out of such things as a deer's ear, bison steaks and sparrows.

He kept his writing-table in the dining-room. When people came to lunch they would find him at it, scribbling away, and it was only with great reluctance that he would get up and take part in the meal. As soon as he had finished eating he would say, 'I am very sorry, now I must get on with my letters.' Even if his guests had not finished their lunch he would leave them to deal with his correspondence. The dining-room had five very smelly aviaries, full of birds, in it, the sort of large zinc structures you see in a zoo. They did not exactly add to the beauty of the decor. The birds were always scratching masses of sand and seed out on to the floor, and mice used to run up and down the legs of the cages as they sought to share in this windfall. There was usually a large tin of meal-worms on a side table with which my father used to feed a pet owl or any other bird due for particular attention.

My early education was completely haphazard. Didi did her best with elementary reading, writing and arithmetic, but I remember no attempt on my father's part to find out what books I was being given and my memory is chiefly of Beatrix Potter and the Christmas annuals. I struggled through masses of Kipling and gave myself nightmares reading Edgar Allan Poe after I had been sent up to bed. I seem to remember innumerable hunting books with stories of deer and wolves, bison and buffalo, but none of them was particularly informative. One of my few pleasures was to spend hours in a far corner of the garden where I could watch the house of our neighbour, a nice admiral named Luard. They were always playing tennis or having parties in their garden and I used to sit on the wall longing to take part. All the other children in the neighbourhood were at school and I simply did not seem to fit in anywhere.

One more orthodox habit my father had retained from his youth was to rent a fishing and shooting estate in Scotland every year. It was in a lovely corner of Galloway, near Newton Stewart, but the house was set in a valley with high hills all round it on which the clouds would sit for months on end. It used to rain every single day. You could motor ten miles in any direction and the sun would be shining. I have never known anything like it. We children had to be ready to leave for the loch at half past eight every morning, wearing ordinary tennis shoes, because my father thought this was good for the growth of our feet, with little spats round our ankles in case we got bitten by adders. We carried a nasty little packet of stringy beef sandwiches and an orange in our pocket and that was our lunch.

We used to set out carrying my father's gaff and an old canvas bag with a lot of flies and things, and then he would fish each pool first and leave us to try our luck after he had thrashed it out. I fished for salmon for thirteen or fourteen years and never felt a fish on the line. My father made quite certain that there was nothing in the pool before he let us try it. It used to bore me to death. My mother had been salmon fishing for ten years with my father and never caught anything either because she had had the same treatment. He was supremely selfish in these ways.

If he caught a trout it would be served to him alone, even if there was quite a large party of people for dinner. The rest of us would be given cod or something more suitable to our status. It was the same with woodcock or snipe. He would have his game bird at the table and everybody else would be given stew or some humbler kind of fare. He would do the same thing if there were guests in the house, not just when the family was present. We used to sit and watch him and think how nice it would be to share these delicacies. Our only common treat was winkles. We used to drive for miles to somewhere on the coast where we would spend half the day collecting them, bring them home, boil them and eat them with a pin.

The boredom of our normal routine was only relieved by two great-aunts, sisters of my grandfather. They both lived in large houses, one at Bexhill and one at Chorley Wood. I think they very much disapproved of the way my grandfather had treated my father and of the way we were brought

41

up. They always had us to stay every year, sometimes twice a year. Both of them lived in a very grand manner, with great houses full of head housemaids and parlour-maids, just as they had been brought up at Woburn. They were just as eccentric as my family is supposed to be. The one at Bexhill was called Lady Ermyntrude Malet and she had peppered the estate with ruins and towers and follies. I have very warm memories of her as she used to give me ten shillings a day pocket-money.

Her sister, Lady Ela Russell, was an old maid who lived entirely alone with her horde of servants. The Chorley Wood house had been built to her own design and when they had finished it they found that they had forgotten to put in a staircase, so half of it had to be torn down again. At one period she had twenty-eight coloured photographs of me in her drawing-room and it was always assumed that I would receive her money when she died. However, I went to lunch there one day and she dashed my hopes by suddenly saying, *à propos* of nothing: 'If ever I make a will I won't leave you a penny, I won't leave you a penny.'

She used to talk to herself a lot. Once when we had been there for about ten days or so, she muttered away at the lunch table: 'Only another four days and then they'll be gone.' There was a girl cousin there on one occasion when my great-aunt suddenly said to herself, very audibly: 'Very nice girl, but intensely stupid, intensely stupid.' At least she was a vicarious source of petty income, as on one visit she gave me sixpence for every mosquito I killed in the house. I made such a fortune that the rate was reduced to a penny a mosquito, but I still have a book saying, 'To John Robert for killing ninety-eight mosquitoes.'

There had been a typical muddle at my christening. My godmother wanted me to be called John and my mother wanted me named Ian. I was registered as John and christened Ian, the name by which I have always been known. Aunt Ela was the only member of the family who used to call me John Robert.

Both great-aunts remained completely Victorian in their

outlook. One year my grandfather took a villa in the south of France for six months and had his two sisters there to stay with him. The day they arrived they went out for a drive and were thrown into consternation at the sight of two Senegalese soldiers. They returned in great haste to report that the whole of the south of France was inhabited by negroes, and said they must go back to England at once before some fate worse than death befell them. The villa was promptly abandoned and left empty for the whole period of the lease.

They did not approve of my grandmother at all and they considered her flying exploits the last straw. One day she had an invitation to fish near Chorley Wood, so she landed her 'plane in Aunt Ela's very large park in order to save time. However, she had not consulted her sister-in-law beforehand and was just making her first cast when she was interrupted by a footman bearing a note from his mistress to say that if she did not remove her aeroplane within half an hour the police would be called to take it away.

The next influence in my life was a tutor, the Reverend Cecil Squire. I started occasional lessons with him about 1927. One of the first consequences of his arrival was the departure of poor old Didi. In my child's mind I blamed him for this, so that I had a grudge and a hatred against him and my parents ever after. He was a fanatic for exercise, and from then on he made my life hell, or at least so I thought at the time. He persuaded my mother that I needed a toughening-up process to make a man of me. So the curious compromise was reached whereby I was sent off to one of the local private schools just to play games.

I really did not understand what was going on most of the time because nobody had explained the games to me and I was made to feel an absolute fool. I suppose I could have got my own back, as a horrible old retired sergeant was hired to give me private boxing lessons. He was an awful man who used to stand there and say 'Hit me in the stomach', and of course when I went into the school gymnasium with the other boys I was so much better at it than they were

43

that I could have knocked them all over the place. They would leave themselves wide open and there was always somebody yelling at me to punch them, but as I hate hurting anybody the result was nothing but confusion.

Life was one appalling round of fencing, boxing, wrestling, rugby and physical jerks. Great-aunt Ela, who also had a house in London, was brought into the plan. I used to go up and stay with her in town and get sent off to a kind of gymnasium place, where they had us climbing up and down ropes and throwing medicine balls in the middle of winter, with all the windows open, ending the session by throwing buckets of cold water all over us. This was all part of the toughening-up process. Riding lessons I minded less, and I became quite good at it, although I was sent to the indoor school at Roehampton when I was very young, where huge men on polo ponies used to ride me against the wall and practically tear my legs off. What good it all did I cannot conceive, apart from putting me off physical exercise for the rest of my life.

In the meantime my father was distinguishing himself by various ill-advised public appearances. In 1923 he had startled his fellow peers by taking the chair at a meeting in support of the Labour candidate for the central division of Portsmouth, although he was careful to explain that he had done so, not because he was a member of the Labour Party, but because he considered the candidate, who was a Quaker acquaintance of his, to be the type of man we needed in Parliament. There was an even worse scandal when he addressed a crowded congregation at the dinner-hour service at St. Martin's Church in the Bullring in Birmingham. About ten people walked out when he said that most British war-time propaganda had been pure fiction and that the Kaiser had never called the British Army a contemptible little army. He also claimed that it was false that the Germans had issued a medal to commemorate the sinking of the *Lusitania*. For all I know he may have been right, but he was so completely contemptuous of public opinion that his forays always got him into trouble.

His principal craze was the Social Credit Movement. He claims in his book that it took him two years, pitting advocates of Social Credit against orthodox economists, before deciding that it provided the key to the solution of the world's major economic troubles. He started propaganda work for the cause and then recorded a comment which is pretty typical of his general attitude: 'It was at this point that I began to experience rather an unpleasant surprise and came up against what, in my later years, has come to be one of life's most worrying discoveries—the Appalling Stupidity of the Ordinary Person.' This became a fixation with him and he used to abbreviate it to A.S.O.T.O.P. and use it as an argument to drive home many of his crack-brained ideas. It was also about this time that he became caught up in the Oxford Group Movement, after going to one of their house parties at Eastbourne.

This was the pattern of his life. Possessions meant nothing to him. He was only interested in animals and birds and fishing and shooting, religious and social movements, which he picked up and then dropped. He was always waving a banner of some kind, peace or monetary reform or something. He was tremendously sincere about it. The only trouble was that he was convinced that he was always right. He was never wrong about anything, he had never made a mistake in his life, which made him very tiresome to live with.

About 1931 the family moved from Portsmouth to an equally unattractive house called Peasmarsh, near Rye. I was vaguely conscious that my parents' marriage, a formal enough affair at the best of times, was disintegrating. My father had taken a dislike to the Reverend Squire and his services had been dispensed with. This decision was taken during our annual pilgrimage to Scotland and provided the only occasion when I saw my mother cry or show any emotion at all. I remember her saying to me how unfair of my father it was to get rid of him and adjuring me to bear in mind how much he had done for me and the family. When we returned home again my mother had some sort of break-down. In a state of some temerity, I remember her asking my father whether she could have enough money to go to the south of France where there was a doctor whom she thought might help her. It was almost the only lengthy conversation between my two parents I ever remember witnessing, but the south of France was entirely out of my father's orbit and she never did go.

Life at Peasmarsh was a repetition of Havant. All the aviaries had been transferred and rebuilt and my father's existence, with its long absences, continued its odd pattern. My brother and sister, some years younger than I was, were looked after by a succession of nurses and maids, and for about a year my mother took over my own education herself. I must confess I cannot remember learning a thing. The chief distraction consisted of catching live flies for a collection of tree frogs my father had bought for my sister. I doubt if she was in the least interested in them, but they multiplied all round the house and used to make life hideous with the warbling noises they made in the middle of the night. Catching live flies is one of the most difficult processes I know, and filling the day's quota used to take hours.

My mother tried to continue the toughening-up process as far as I was concerned. There was one dreadful episode when I was sent off to play golf at Rye in midwinter. You get a north-east wind whistling across the course—there is practically nothing between Rye and Siberia in the winter, I've never known such a ghastly place. I drove my ball off, and the wind was so biting that my eyes were streaming with tears. I could not see where I was but I went off vaguely to look for the ball. When I came back the wind had killed off some poor old man on the way down, and he was dying on my overcoat in the club-house. They had rolled it into a pillow for his head and I had to wait two or three hours before I got my coat back. I could not leave because it was so hideously cold and I did not like to whip it out from under his head while he lay dying.

I very seldom saw my father. We had absolutely nothing in common. He has written himself that his own parents

46

were disappointed in him because he did not share any particular skill in which they would have liked him to excel. The same was absolutely true in my case. I was never in the least interested in birds or animals or his peace projects. He put me off religion with his militant ideas for a long time. All I could see was the Bible-thumping and the hypocrisy and his whole outlook did not seem to ring true. During his brief incursions I was subjected to the usual talks about the facts of life. I used to get an hour on bestiality, and an hour on the subject of the Gospel according to St. Mark, but I could never take his instruction seriously. Now I look back, he talked about the teachings of the Bible with great warmth and understanding, but I was never able to separate him from what he was propounding and the lessons did not sink home.

The talks on sex were given in a flat, impartial fashion, with no information barred, but it was all very strange and completely impersonal. All he did was to evoke my curiosity without emphasizing the dangers. 'I have never been tempted in this direction myself,' he would say, 'but I can quite understand people being so'—these homilies on sex and religion acquired a completely unreal air in what was already a broken home and it is hardly surprising that I derived little benefit from them.

The only really pleasant contacts I can remember at the time were a family named Scott, who had a big place not far from Peasmarsh. The father, as I recall, was a wealthy stock-broker. They had their own cricket ground, used to go hunting and entertain a lot and they were very kind and hospitable to me. The daughter of the house had broken her back out hunting and had become a semi-invalid. She was a charming, intelligent girl and, I think, was pleased to have someone to talk to. My visits there enabled me to escape from the awful, carping atmosphere at home, and I spent long periods with the Scotts, who always had amusing people staying at the house. They knew and talked about the London scene and gave me an insight into the sort of life of which I had been completely deprived up till then.

47

My memory of the exact chronology of my existence at the time is understandably confused. In due course I was confided to the care of a new tutor, with whom I made a number of semi-educational visits abroad. I went on a liner cruise to Scandinavia with him, but the details are hazy. I remember the china factory, and the Tivoli Gardens at Copenhagen, and one fjord looking exactly like another; also a most extraordinary and very smelly night-club in Hamburg full of naked women galloping round an arena on horseback. I was also a victim of my father's enthusiasm for the Oxford Group Movement. They were holding some sort of rally at Oxford during the vacation, taking over a number of colleges for the purpose. At least it gave me a fairly catholic introduction to the subject of sex. There was a horrible fat Buchmanite who tried to make homosexual advances to me, and I succeeded, to my great delight, in finding my first girl-friend. It was quite a fortnight.

Then came a brief interlude of greater order. My father arranged for me to go and live with his old friend Canon Raven at Ely. It was rather a pleasant old house, although freezing cold like every other house I had lived in since the day I was born. It was full of stone flags, refectory tables and rush seats and I have never known people drink quite so much tea. They used to have early-morning tea and tea for breakfast, tea in the middle of the day, tea after lunch, tea for tea, tea after dinner and tea before they went to bed.

I did not see much of the good canon, but he was in fact the agent of my first visit to Woburn. I had been completely baffled by the intelligence I had received from the little parlour-maid about my connexion with the Bedford family and the atmosphere at Peasmarsh was such that I had not dared to broach the subject to my father or mother. I felt there must be some sinister piece of family history which it would be unwise to bring up. However I did talk about it to Canon Raven and it was he who took the initiative in writing to my father and thus started the chain of events which led to my paying the first visit to our ancestral home.

In my youthful enthusiasm I had tried to effect some reconciliation between my father and grandfather, but I would have done better to spare myself the trouble. They did in fact meet again, although I was never present. They both seemed to have made up their mind, even when I was only sixteen, that I was likely to prove an unsatisfactory heir and they put their heads together to alter the terms of the entail on the Bedford estate to my detriment. It was pure and utter malice on their part. They just wanted to tie everything up in small knots. Neither of them had any power in the world other than the power of money. It was the only way they could appeal to or control people and they always exploited it. The net result was that instead of being appointed tenant for life of the estate, they appointed trustees for life in my place. This was at no time revoked and it is the main reason why I find myself in the position I am in to-day.

I was by now in the hands of another tutor, a rugger-playing type studying to become a lawyer. Most of the day was spent with him trying to cram me full of sufficient knowledge to pass the entrance exams into Cambridge. After the extraordinary life I had been obliged to lead it is no wonder that I had no particular interest in acquiring it, so the whole project was doomed from the start. I was playing a certain amount of tennis and riding, which I enjoyed. One of the Raven daughters used to teach folk-dancing to the local ladies of Ely, and I was roped in. I must say I have never laughed so much.

However, at least I was meeting other people of my own age for the first time in my life. I started to get to know quite a number of undergraduates at the university and usually disappeared from the house every evening to attend some drinking party or other, arriving back at all hours, with the result that I usually had a shocking hangover when the tutor tried to concentrate my mind on my studies again. Never having been subjected to the normal discipline of school life, it was inevitable that I should kick over the traces at the first opportunity. As I was to find out, if you do not go to school, you do not get your bottom kicked early enough. All the kicking comes later and it hurts much more.

Looking back, I fear I must have been a pretty unpleasant young fellow, and very difficult to get along with. The Raven *ménage* was much more sober-minded than my more raffish Cambridge friends. I went off one winter on my first skiing holiday with a small party one of the Raven daughters had organized. It was formed of the sort of bright, enthusiastic young people who get up at seven-thirty and are always first on the ski-lift in the morning and last down at night, terribly hearty, brash, slap-on-the-back people with whom I had no contact at all. I used to turn up on the slopes at ten, and after two or three days they gave me up as a bad job. The journey out had been thoroughly embarrassing. We had travelled third-class, which I hated, sitting up all night in extreme discomfort, and there was some bright young man, the natural organizer type, who was bossing us all around. He used to undertip the porters and there was one terrible scene when he had given a French porter fifty francs for moving about twenty suitcases, the sort of stinginess I cannot abide.

At home, things had gone from bad to worse. In the end my mother found my father impossible and there was a very unpleasant court case involving their legal separation. The first sign I remember of her showing some spirit of independence was when she went out and bought herself a whole wardrobe full of new clothes, something she had never had in her whole life. All at once she began to wear garments that were recognizably fashionable, started using lipstick, playing games and visiting her neighbours, where previously she had just sat around the house. My father's reaction was to have an official notice published saying that he expressly withdrew all authority for any person to pledge his credit.

Then, in 1935, my mother sued my father for restitution of conjugal rights, saying that he had deserted her. He in turn pleaded that he was justified in refusing to cohabit with his wife. The case was the talk of London at the time, with my father being defended by Sir Patrick Hastings and Norman Birkett, and my mother being represented by Mr. Roland Oliver.

Although they were careful to say that there was no suggestion that my mother had committed misconduct, my father's lawyers put forward the case that my tutor had obtained too much influence over my mother and that she had become estranged from her husband. She, for her part, claimed that there was nothing to justify her husband leaving her and that there was no impropriety in her relations with Mr. Squire.

However, the petition was dismissed, although the judge quoted a letter in court which must be recorded. Mr. Justice Bucknill commented:

> The social views of Lord Tavistock are fairly summed up in letters written by one of his relatives in which it was stated that Lord Tavistock has very high ideals and lives up in the clouds. He has a colossal sense of Christian duty to his fellow men, which tends to make him more difficult to deal with than a normal person. Lord Tavistock takes a rigid and austere view of life and dislikes many things, some of which he calls pagan, but which most men do not actively dislike. He dislikes boarding-schools for boys, alcohol, tobacco, playing cards for money and betting. He does not play games and says he took very little interest in his wife's clothes.

The case cost them something like twenty thousand pounds.

By now I was sufficiently grown-up to see that I was going to have to try and organize my life without much affection or help from my family. My father had moved into a depressing little flat in St. James's Court, where I was subjected to one of the most squalid episodes of an unpleasant childhood. He had written to say that he wanted me to call in one evening and read through the contents of a despatch case which he had left out for me. It was full of singularly unattractive letters between my father and mother plus a lot of evidence taken on affidavit from the servants concerning the alleged relationship between her and my tutor. I cannot think what his motives were in bringing out all this dirty linen, except that in his usual obsessive way I suppose he was trying to whitewash himself and put my mother in the wrong.

From then on I saw very little of either of them. My mother stayed on first at Peasmarsh and then bought a smaller property near by. My father acquired another house near Haywards Heath. It was an awful villa with gables, a really dreadful place, full of linoleum all up the stairs and along the passages, like a boarding-house. It was the sort of dwelling he was used to, and typical of the sort of houses his friends lived in. I went there as little as possible and my contact with both of them degenerated into desultory visits and correspondence, although my father did attempt to control the general pattern of my existence for the next two or three years.

I realized only too well what I had been missing with the miserable, provincial life I had lived with my parents, and was delighted when my father decided to remove me from the Raven establishment, and deposit me with a friend of his named Mrs. Osborne Samuel, who ran a sort of polyglot boarding-house for overseas students in Bloomsbury. This was about the beginning of 1936, when I was nineteen. From then on, I was more or less on my own.

CHAPTER THREE

TUTORS AND HOSTESSES

I WAS consigned to this Bloomsbury students' hostel and left more or less to my own devices on an allowance of ninety-eight pounds a year. This may sound princely enough, but I had a title; the word soon got around whose son and grandson I was, and it was apparently expected of the eventual heir of an estate worth several million pounds to keep up some sort of appearance. My father seemed to think that I would acquire some of his conceptions of brotherly love amidst this odd collection of Indian and Chinese and Egyptian students, but of course we all hated the sight of each other. They were all working furiously for London University degrees and, apart from our communal breakfasts and communal dinners, I saw very little of them.

Mrs. Samuel had known my father for some years. They had been associated in one of his social welfare schemes, and I think he had helped her buy the lease of this Bloomsbury house. They were seeing less of each other at the time and I suspect that his paying for my board and lodging was a way of maintaining their relationship without too many obligations on his part. He used to turn up very occasionally and sometimes stay the night, issue some fulminating edict on my way of life, but otherwise made little further attempt to organize it in detail. In a desultory way, chiefly in the hope of ingratiating myself with my new-found grandfather, I made another effort to study for the Cambridge entrance exams at a firm of crammers, but as my mind had never been taught to learn anything it was a sorry process.

One of my most pleasant recollections of this otherwise frustrating period was the kindness of some older cousins named Sir Claude and Lady Russell. He had been in the diplomatic service, minister in Portugal, Abyssinia and elsewhere, had just retired and was living in London. I believe one of my great-aunts had written to them to say that this young nephew was on his own in London, and would they try and look after me. I could not have asked for nicer foster-parents. Without making it in any way obtrusive, they gave me a lot of good advice—I wish now I had paid more heed to it—and tried to make up for the lack of affection and the crass ignorance of my family and its history which was all I had to show for my connexion with it at the age of eighteen or nineteen. There I was, stuck in this depressing Bloomsbury establishment, to all intents and purposes uneducated, only on terms of spasmodic and formal contact with my parents and grandparents, and left very largely to my own devices. The life of a lord, as far as I was concerned, was about as barren as it could possibly be. It was probably the fault of a character I had had little enough opportunity to form, but I had few interests, less incentives and was filled with probably unreasonable resentment against what seemed to me the manner in which my family had washed their hands of me. I was torn between outright revolt and a realization that I ought to make an effort to get myself educated, and pass the entrance exams into university and the new-found charms of London life.

Sir Claude Russell had not only tried to instil some knowledge of my family, but felt that this young Bedford sprig ought to make his way in the society to which he nominally belonged. Part of his many kindnesses was to put me in touch with the leading hostesses of the day, Lady Cunard, Lady Londonderry, the Duchess of Rutland, Lady Anglesey, Lady Astor, Lady Moyne and many others. I suppose I came under the heading of an available, if not particularly eligible young bachelor and was a useful chair-stopper when they found they needed to fill up a lunch or dinner table. I was the only member of my family who had been seen around town for three generations, so I imagine I had a sort of curiosity value. Why they bothered I cannot think. I was terribly unsure of myself and in self-defence used to adopt a consciously languid air and go round wearing a monocle. I must have been an insufferable young man.

Needless to say, I was enchanted by the whole process. I had never really met any social contemporaries before that time. One would get on to a sort of list and receive invitations from people one had never met, often going on to supper after, almost forgetting whom one had had dinner with. I was wined and dined, made the round of the town houses and then started getting invitations to their country estates. On ninety-eight pounds a year it was like manna from heaven, although I did a lot of walking from Blooms-bury Square to Belgravia to save the bus fare.

I found myself going to concerts and theatres and operas, something I had never done before. I had never heard any serious music or been conscious of artistic life at all and the whole round took my fancy enormously. I suppose any-one is sufficient of a snob to enjoy moving in high society. To me it was something new, exciting and comfortable. The food was good and the people were amusing. The only trouble was it took up more and more of my time, and although I tried to work in a certain amount of study before lunch and in the evening before I went out, I must admit the educational side of my activities started to suffer.

There was one moment of conscience when I decided that I must start earning my living. I think the necessity for extra cash was the main reason, but of all things my mind lighted on dress designing as a career. Why, I am simply at a loss to explain, and in fact was baffled to find references to it when I looked through my papers. I went to some sort of training school in Bond Street, where there was a poor woman called Miss Smith who used to have to carry out my ideas. These may have been prompted by suddenly seeing my mother blossom into fashionable clothes after all the years of wearing home-made sacks.

This phase did not last very long, but curiously enough my father did not seem to object when he heard of it:

'Providing it is not fundamentally a rotten career or profession (like the army!)' he wrote in one of his peculiar homilies, 'a man can make good in the fullest sense doing almost anything. A good many people will look down on you because of the career you are choosing, but you will have weighed that up by now and I don't think they are people who count much in God's sight, although they will, some of them, be people who cut a good deal of ice in the high social circles you are apt to frequent.'

This sort of long distance nagging would go on from time to time. The following effusion gives a good idea of the way his mind worked:

You have a Whitwell strain in you and Gangye (that was the family nickname for my maternal grandmother) alas is not a hopeful ancestress. I have seen her appalling snobbishness, her selfishness, her weakness and her habit of shirking anything that calls for effort or sacrifice come out in the lives of her children and unless they face the tendency and fight it, it will spoil the lives of her grandchildren as well.

Judging from my own past recollections and from what I hear and see of them to-day, most society people, with some noteworthy exceptions, of which your friend Lady Astor would seem to be one, are a rather poor crowd, wasting time, life and money on trivial things and at the present moment, when such grave things are happening or threatening to happen, fiddling both rashly and also contemptuously while Rome is burning.

Unfortunately there seem hardly any men holding important positions at the present moment who show much vision, moral courage or sound judgment. I heard old Mr. Lansbury (who of course is not one of the upper ten) speaking the other day and was impressed by the fact that he was so obviously streets ahead in character and outlook of any younger, more active and more influential politician with greater advantages of birth.

In your inmost heart you still keep a rather remote

but quite real respect for Christ, but in much of your life and in many of your words you in effect say 'Christ is an ass and I know better than He'. It is because every year I live I grow more sure that Christ is not an ass and that those who live as though he were are heading for trouble, that I do not feel like giving you all you want in certain ways.

I remember answering the first part of that by asking whether he accepted no share of the responsibility in my birth or whether I was another example of immaculate conception.

Where my father wrote long diatribes which never failed to invoke the Deity, my grandfather, with whom I had also entered into a desultory correspondence, wrote the most extraordinary letters I have ever seen penned. They seldom took up more than fifteen or twenty words on one side of a small four-fold piece of paper. Two typical examples at the time read:

I am sorry for you not caring for shooting and fishing and the sports of the field and the moor as you ought. A sad falling off from former generations of your family.

*　　*　　*　　*

I am pleased to hear that you like riding and hunting, that is something to the good. Horse-racing, when you do not own horses and do not know the horses running, is simply betting and gambling, which you had better avoid. As for greyhound-racing, that is not fit to be touched in any way and I trust you will not go so low down as that in your pursuits.

I had also written rather tentatively to ask if a slightly greater share of the family wealth might not come my way. The reply was crushing:

You ask me to suggest to your father the increasing of your allowance by two hundred and fifty pounds a year. You talk of people of your own class—boys of your own class, except that they are coasters, go to a university and acquire the education and training you will lack and which will mark you in later life as an ill-educated man. You are doing nothing and not attempting to qualify for any profession. My opinion is that your father is treating you too generously.

He was of course quite right, and I must have made some attempt to pull myself together. More as a means of getting into his good books than anything else, I decided I would go to a firm of crammers and make one last attempt to pass the Cambridge exams. I was recommended, I think by Mrs. Samuel, to a firm called Scoones, which operated near the British Museum. This brought a wintry response from the old duke in three more of his letters:

> I am pleased to hear from you that you are willing and anxious to try and get into Cambridge. That is the best thing I have heard about you.

*   *   *   *

> I think you are right in going to the firm of Scoones. I will pay all their fees and charges and if you pass into the university as I hope you will, I will then give you an adequate allowance for an undergraduate at Cambridge.

*   *   *   *

> You mention the Encyclopædia Britannica as a useful book of reference. So it is—but it is an enormous work and could take up many shelves of a large bookcase. It is also costly, but I expect a second-hand copy could be bought. I will make enquiries and write to you again.

Alas for good intentions, the mood did not last long. It is a rare tutor who can impart interest to the disinterested, and my trouble was that I had never even learnt to learn. However I ploughed on for a time, but much preferred the gay company of my hostesses.

Lady Cunard was my favourite. She still ran the most lavish *salon* in London and had a corner house in Grosvenor

Square, which has just been turned into a block of flats. She was an extraordinarily vital person and tremendously well informed. She used to read voraciously, hardly ever slept, and had a habit of ringing people up at three or four in the morning with some bright idea that had entered her head. She had a remarkable memory for names and for music, of which she could sing long excerpts. If the conversation turned that way, she would immediately sing the melody in question, or if a certain book was mentioned, she could quote long phrases from it. At the same time she took a great interest in everything that was new, and in all things young, particularly young people. You could meet anybody at her parties from Conservative ministers to Gertrude Stein, writers and newspaper people to most of the dukes and duchesses in the land. She was a great schemer of romances and always produced or took under her protection the latest couple being talked about.

The conversation used to range over the whole field of politics and the arts, and to make any sense in these surroundings I had to read up quite a bit. In fact it was a very much better education than I ever got from my tutors. She would start the ball rolling by tossing some conversational bomb or bouquet to draw people out and make them talk. The particular bomb for me was always, 'This poor penniless boy and this millionaire duke of a grandfather.' Her parties were generally built round a particular person or a particular idea. It might be a musical evening or Mrs. Simpson. There was one occasion I remember when her musical memory let her down. Sir Thomas Beecham and the London Philharmonic Orchestra had been invited *en bloc* and half-way through the concert she went up to Sir Thomas and said: 'You haven't played my favourite piece.' 'Madam,' he replied, 'I've just played it.'

The only sort of return I could make for this hospitality was to worm his Covent Garden box out of my grandfather, and place it at Lady Cunard's disposal. She usually had the royal box herself and used to use ours as an overflow. There was one awful occasion when my share of the guests included Mrs. Simpson. I took them off down a passage which I assumed communicated between the two boxes and found that I had led them all into the royal lavatory.

Every coterie has its eccentrics on the fringe. A very rich American woman named Mabel Cory used to appear at Lady Cunard's parties from time to time and gather up various people from them for her own lunches and dinners. She was a millionairess several times over but she was afflicted with a strange sort of meanness. She used to walk everywhere all over London, long distances such as from Grosvenor Square to South Kensington, in order not to waste money on taxis. She stayed at Claridges, and three-quarters of the way through the meal used to have the rest of her lunch sent up to her room so that she could eat it in the evening. I believe she had a château outside Paris, where she was always suspecting the servants of stealing things. She used to hide money all over the place and then not be able to find it. Some poor servant would be threatened with the sack and it used to turn up in some obscure hiding-place days later.

The Dowager Duchess of Rutland was a sweet old lady who kept the sort of house where all kinds of lost souls like myself could forgather. She would put herself out to understand their problems and difficulties. Numbers of odd and amusing people dropped in and the number of lame ducks she looked after was astronomical. She was always convinced that her flocks of geese were swans. She was for ever helping people, singers who couldn't sing, artists who couldn't draw or paint, introducing them to people who might help them.

I could always go to her house in Chapel Street and get the odd meal and be sure of meeting someone interesting or amusing. In the end she practically had it knocked down and rebuilt for Lady Diana Cooper, with an enormous library for Duff Cooper to keep all his books in. Brenda, Lady Dufferin was another old lady who used to take pity on me and sometimes had me to stay at her house in Wiltshire. I believe she even bought some of my terrible dress designs to help me out, but I don't think she ever had the nerve to have them made up.

But it was Marjorie Anglesey who provided me with the nearest approach to a home I had at the time. They were a charming pair with a large family of five or six children, and handsome houses in London and in Wales. I used to stay there a lot and would go round more or less whenever I liked for lunch or dinner at the town house in Queen's Gate. The Marquess was a gentleman-in-waiting to Queen Mary and he had a mania for building. They had builders in their lovely house in Anglesey, Plâs-newydd, for something like eight years. He had very good taste and had Rex Whistler paint a dining-room for him when the artist was relatively unknown.

This was fringe-of-Court society rather than political or musical, and they used to have big house-parties at Plâs-newydd during most of August and September. It was right on an estuary in a beautiful position and, although the entertaining was very informal, it was on a very grand scale. Plâs-newydd was one of the most comfortable houses I have ever known, everything was beautifully done, every single thing was thought of. The style was so lavish that even they used to have to economize occasionally, and this usually took the form of giving up their supply of Malvern water. They used to spend about three hundred pounds a year on bath essence and burning incense round the house.

In spite of my father's grudging approval, I did not fit into Lady Astor's set very well. I remember staying at Cliveden for one Ascot week, although I did not have enough money for my royal enclosure voucher and the present Lord Astor very generously paid for it. I arrived about six o'clock and found that there was a huge house-party staying, either very old Americans and racing people or very young things who all seemed to know one another, but none of whom I had met. Nobody spoke to me and I hung around until dinner-time, went up and changed, came down to dinner and still no one spoke to me. The two girls on either side of me knew each other very well, talked across me as if I was not there. When they went out with the port neither of them had spoken to me and after dinner no one spoke to me. So about ten o'clock I went up to bed without having spoken to a soul.

I had just settled down with a book when about ten of these young people arrived to make me an apple-pie bed. When they saw I was already ensconced they rather shame-facedly asked me if I had a headache and whether I wanted some aspirin. Their arms were chock-a-block with needles and lumps of coal, holly and all the other paraphernalia for their silly little rag, which they quickly pushed in the background. I stayed in the house for three or four days and during that time I do not think I exchanged more than three or four words with anybody. I had never been more miserable in the whole of my life.

The Astors also used to give big parties in London, with lavish entertainment, but as Lady Astor disapproved of people drinking, the only place to get gin, or whisky and soda was in the butler's pantry. No wine was served with meals and no alcohol of any sort. Unless one had *entrée* to the butler's pantry, or to the coachman in the stables, it was a completely dry occasion.

I blotted my copy-book very badly at another very grand house belonging to Lord Bradford. All the house guests were bridge fiends and used to play all day long from about ten o'clock onwards. Even at sixpence and a shilling a hundred this was hell for me on ninety-eight pounds a year, and when they started playing for ten-shilling or pound stakes, someone had to carry me. I had taken a dreadful pornographic book down with me as light relief and a very characterful old lady named Lady Ancaster asked if she could borrow it. Unfortunately I had left my name written in it, and she left it behind, so I never got invited to that house again.

This must all sound a pretty foppish and useless life, but for me it had a tremendous fascination. I had never been in the Ritz Hotels and grand houses of the world and seen huge amounts of money spent on clothes and jewellery, and having a good time. The trouble was I had nowhere to invite anybody in return. My mother lived in this freezing cold house near Rye, where the doors and windows were always open, the food disgusting, and I was ashamed to take anybody there. My father was by now installed in his Victorian monstrosity at Haywards Heath and it was simply not the sort of place to which I could take any of my new friends.

He was surrounded by sycophants and vicars' wives, all terribly smug Bible-thumpers with prayers and colly-wobbles before breakfast. It was a frightful atmosphere, with everybody gabbling about godliness, and very little of it in action, apart from pandering to my father and telling him what a marvellous man he was. If the conversation was not about religion, it was on the subject of ornithology or Douglas Social Credit. He must always have been the same way. I remember Lady Anglesey telling me that when she was a débutante and he a young man she sat next to him at a dinner-party. The only thing he could find to talk about were the habits of flies, which, as a bright young thing, she found an extremely tricky subject to discuss.

My grandfather still kept up the two houses in Belgrave Square for his twice-yearly attendance at the meetings of the Zoological Society, but I never went near them. Nevertheless he had slightly more inkling of the sort of life into which I was being introduced than my father: 'As the autumn approaches people go country-house visiting,' he wrote me during 1936. 'This I know is expensive in many ways. As you have gone to Scoones and have I hope made some progress towards the university, I shall be glad to make country-house visiting for you possible. I suggest giving you a cheque for five pounds for each house you stay at, provided you tell me where you are going to stay and that I have no objection to the people who have asked you. I am looking out for a second-hand encyclopædia for you but one has not yet turned up.'

Approval in his case meant such houses as the Londonderries and the Moynes. A couple of weeks later he was writing again: 'Your shortest way to Lord Londonderry's is London via Stranraer to Belfast. Return fare seven pounds ten with sleeping berth. If you choose a more expensive route that is your affair. I therefore send you a cheque for twelve pounds ten. You will have no tips to give to servants at Lord Londonderry's, which is a great blessing. My father and your great-grandfather was the first to abolish giving tips by visitors to servants in his house.'

My visit to the Londonderry establishment at Mount Stewart in Northern Ireland was not an unqualified success. I staggered off the night-boat on which I had been frightfully sick, and immediately I arrived they said they were going yacht-racing. I had never been yacht-racing, nor on a yacht of any size before, so I jumped into the necessary clothes and we set off. We were doing very well, in fact I think we were winning and suddenly they all shouted at me to let go the something-or-other. So I let go the nearest bit of rope that came to hand and it let down the mast. I had always regarded Lady Londonderry as a very grand respectable gentlewoman, and had seen her at Londonderry House at most formal parties. Her flow of language on this occasion was a source of delight to me.

Lord Londonderry used to get up very early in the morning and fly round and round the house at about half past six in his aeroplane. They also had a pipe band patrolling round the house at dawn and round the dinner-table at night, where of course the hideous noise stopped all conversation. I never did solve the tipping problem. At Woburn my grandfather had left printed notes everywhere telling guests not to tip the servants, but at Mount Stewart there was no such helpful advice, so in the end I left nothing, hoping for the best.

The Moynes had a house in Grosvenor Place, another in Hampstead and a further odd conglomeration of old buildings near Littlehampton. It was the fashion to go there for Goodwood. It was a most fantastic house, because

64

everything had to be as nature wished it. You arrived and thought it must be deserted because there was no proper drive. There were weeds growing everywhere, moss planted on the roof, nothing like a front-door bell and it was terribly difficult to find your way about. No cultivated flowers were allowed. There were huge bowls of weeds everywhere, cow parsley and grasses and bulrushes. Anybody subject to hay fever sneezed his head off the whole time. Nothing grew very well in the sandy soil, so that cow parsley and dandelions were cultivated under bits of wire to protect them. There were oak trees tied up with dozens of bits of wire to make them grow where they had no intention of growing at all.

When you got into the house you found it a very odd mixture. A bleak ground floor with genuine fourteenth-century settles and chairs of the period all over the place, while the upstairs was tricked out with four-poster beds and beautiful bathrooms and every possible luxury. I arrived just before dinner, and was waiting all by myself when suddenly someone swept in wearing a most enormous dress. I leapt to my feet and she asked whether I would like some sherry. I thought it was some friend or relation and said 'Thank you very much,' and we carried on rather a stilted conversation before she swept out again.

It was not until everyone came down for dinner that I realized the person I had been talking to was the parlour-maid. They were all dressed up in fancy dress of the period with wimples and huge grey dresses sweeping the ground. It was a terribly grand house-party with an absolute covey of duchesses. I always remember the Duchess of Buccleuch and the Duchess of Northumberland sidling through the door together in their determination not to give precedence to the other.

Lord and Lady Moyne lived very much their own separate lives. The house was really two houses with a tunnel between them. Layd Moyne lived on one side of the tunnel and he and the children lived on the other. For some reason she took a great fancy to me and I used to spend most of my time in her part of the house with her, tearing all the house guests apart. Back in London she was very kind. She thought I was starving on the Bloomsbury boarding-house food, and used to send me round puddings from Gunter's and little parcels of dishes and pies. Mrs. Samuel was not exactly pleased as she took it as a reflection on her establishment.

The most extraordinary house I have ever stayed at, one that would certainly not have been approved of by my grandfather, belonged to Lord Tredegar, down in South Wales. He was a papal count of some sort and lived surrounded exclusively by Great Danes and handsome menservants. I was taken there, I add hastily, by Lady Cunard. He really was an extraordinary fellow, with altars all over the house and a somewhat terrifying interest in black magic.

He told somebody's fortune one night in his bedroom. There were three or four of us sitting in front of a huge fire, with the flames flickering on the four-poster bed. There was an owl flying round the room, and our host had put on some clothes which were supposed to have belonged to some witch in the past, and was holding up the skeleton of a witch's hand. While he was telling this fortune the temperature of the room fell so much that I was absolutely freezing in front of this enormous fire. It was one of the most eerie experiences I have ever had.

It was a most odd establishment. Leaping all round the park there were kangaroos and things that he used to fend off with a stick. His notions of hospitality were pretty bizarre. One of the evenings we were there he settled his house-party of twenty or thirty people down to dinner and then went off to some regimental or local do, abandoning his guests to carry on as best they could. He had asked in some Welsh singers to entertain us during dinner. They stood outside the dining-room windows, which we had to keep open. In the end freezing to death in the icy draught, we got up and shut them, leaving the Welsh singers burbling on happily outside. Folk-songs are not exactly the ideal accompaniment to a meal.

Lady Cunard was the only one of us who was civil enough to go out and thank them. Lord Tredegar then came back from what had obviously been a liquid occasion, and flew into a terrible rage when he discovered that we had shut the windows on his favourite choir. He and Lady Cunard had a stand-up row and she threatened to leave, although the whole thing was patched up again in the morning.

He had a town house in Grosvenor Square where his mother lived. She, poor thing, thought she was a bird. She used to flit round the house with sticks and straws in her mouth making birds' nests, and then sit on eggs herself and try to hatch them. It was by all odds the most peculiar family I have ever come across.

Not all my acquaintances were as eccentric as this. Lord Granard, who had been a friend of my grandfather's and a master of the horse or something when the old duke had been a gentleman-in-waiting to King George V, also took an interest in me. He was very shocked at the way in which I was forced to live on ninety-eight pounds a year in London because his son, Lord Forbes, who was up at Cambridge at the time, was one of the few undergraduates who had a Rolls and a chauffeur with him, and lived in a very different state. At one point he wrote to my grandfather and said that the way I was being brought up was monstrous.

The old gentleman had his own ideas on the subject, probably not without reason. Towards the end of the year he wrote me one of his longest letters:

> I hear from Scoones that they advise your going up for the first entrance exam for Cambridge next December and the second in March. But they add 'that neither principals nor tutors will accept any responsibility for future progress unless some radical change is made in his way of life and that regular homework is done and in addition that regular hours of sleep are kept.' If you fail then of course no increase will be made until you do so. I shall certainly not help you again. Your choice is between passing exams which anyone with an ordinary education

67

can easily do and getting a good allowance or failing to do so and living on a very scanty yearly pittance.

He was by no means blind to my past troubles. 'I quite allow that you have not had a useful education up till the present,' he was writing a few days later, 'but that makes it all the more necessary that you should now, when you have the chance, turn to and do all you can to make up for lost time. I am glad you have sent in the Trinity College entrance exam form.'

I must have put in a few sessions of midnight oil, as I see from a complete missive in December: 'I am very glad to hear you have passed the first part of your exam and congratulate you upon it.' Three days later he wrote again: 'I send enclosed cheque for twenty-five pounds to reward you for your success in your exam and encourage you for further exertions.'

His terse comment on Edward VIII's abdication came in the middle of all this: 'After the late King's good record his failure in his duty to the Empire is deplorable. He puts himself first and the Empire second. In a short time remorse must come and he will realize his mistake and have a miserable time.'

That twenty-five pounds went on a skiing holiday, not, praise be, a repetition of the hearty affair organized by Canon Raven's daughter, but a much more sophisticated party arranged by Chris Mackintosh, one of the big figures in skiing at the time, and his sister Lady Margaret Drummond-Hay. We went to Scheidegg and this time I thoroughly enjoyed it, although I tore the muscles in a knee in a bad fall. That was not the main incident of the holiday. Shortly after I arrived I had skied down the valley with the intention of taking the last train back, but I missed it. So I decided to walk back up the line and on the way it started to snow, soon thickening into a blizzard. I stayed in one of the tunnels on the line between Grindelwald and Scheidegg and sheltered there half the night, frozen to death, terrified and surrounded by dripping water. Of course they had sent out tremendous search-parties in all directions and I was by no means popular.

Back home I fear success had gone to my head. I really felt I could not face the crammers again and they gave me up as a bad job. I had only gone there in the first place to please my father and grandfather, and felt that all I was getting in return was frigid homilies. There was probably very little that is praiseworthy in my attitude, but they had both kept me at arm's length all my life and I used to have moods of feeling that they were just not worth pleasing. Looking back, however, it is difficult to cavil with the little note—the whole letter by the way—I received from my grandfather on the occasion: 'Scoones will not continue teaching you because you will not work—they have therefore given you up. There is no doubt about the matter at all.'

My father and grandfather had seen each other several times by now, although I never received any of the credit for bringing them together again. I was never present during any of these encounters and used to hear garbled versions through other members of the family. No attempt was made to rake up old grievances and they spent most of their time talking about the weather or the crops. The atmosphere was clearly at once electric and defensive. I imagine my father was frightened of my grandfather, who could be a very frightening man. They just had these formal conversations because neither of them could talk any other way. I do not think there was ever any paternal or filial feeling where my father and grandfather were concerned. Neither of them was capable of expressing any emotion, it was quite beyond them. The capacity for expressing affection of any sort was something quite lacking from their temperaments.

I maintained desultory contact with my mother, whose opinion of the Russell side of the family had not been improved by events: 'I am so sorry we can't come to the opera tomorrow,' I find one letter of hers saying. 'I take it very kindly you should have asked us and we would greatly have liked to go with you. At the same time I have a prejudice against taking any favours even remotely connected with the old man so I would prefer not to go in the box.'

With my grandmother, on the other hand, I had struck up an occasional correspondence that was almost cosy by contrast. Even she did not seem to realize that the sort of standards expected around London of a young man with a title could not possibly be maintained on the sort of allowance I was receiving. I remember I wrote to say that I had to have three decent new shirts which would cost me three pounds each and would she help me buy them. She wrote back a long lecture saying that people should be plainly and simply dressed and that she simply could not understand shirts costing three pounds, so I never got them. And yet she had an annual income of thirty thousand pounds a year and had spent fortunes in her youth on her Court dresses.

There was something very revealing in one of our earlier exchanges, in which we were talking about the way I had been brought up:

I know very little about your early life as you are probably aware, but from what I have heard from outsiders (mostly relations) you have had tutors ever since you were of school age, except when your mother taught you for two years and you have disliked all. . . . You ask why I did not give my son the education I recommend for you 'if I think it is so good'. I had nothing whatever to do with your father's education; it was taken entirely out of my hands. At the age of one month his grandparents altered all the arrangements I made for him and continued to preside till they died, after which your grandfather and Miss Greene entirely ruled matters and I was not permitted even to know what was being done. I was entertained for a night in Africa during one of my flights by the Governor of a province who told me that he had been tutor to my son for a time. I had never even heard of him! . . .

Your father came under influence at Oxford which showed him a way of devoting his life to work for others instead of thinking only of himself, his likes and dislikes. He also fell deeply in love with a girl who at the time seemed to have kindred tastes. It has been a grievous disappointment to find that she has ceased to care for him and the work in which he was so deeply interested and has moreover (he firmly believes) been otherwise unfaithful to him. . . .

You cannot expect your father to make you a large allowance when your mother has recklessly run him into debt and even now may be making things more and more difficult, as I believe he is responsible for her lawyers' fees if she does not pay them herself.

She certainly had reservations about the family she had married into. We had been comparing the merits of Copenhagen china in one of our exchanges and she commented:

Yes, one wants very delicate surrounds for anything so delicate as the Copenhagen pottery, but I like it so much that till I have a furnished house of my own it will have to suffer what I am convinced has been a succession of Russells with no artistic tastes whatsoever for two or three hundred years. When I say no artistic tastes I mean only a respect for portraits by good painters and bits of furniture which cost a lot and no innate artistic feeling. The furnishing of the Abbey is enough to make artistic angels weep.

She found her son a distinct trial:

I have just been telling your father that when I see a thick letter from him, I get the same sinking feeling below my pinafore that I used to when my mother wrote to me, because I know I am going to get a lecture and a scolding. However I added that with him I had the satisfaction of answering back. As I have been so much deafer since I had the 'flu', correspondence is now almost my only way of keeping contact with my fellow creatures.

71

I really felt quite sorry for her. She was a rather sad old lady before the end. She was still getting in the news with her flying trips and on one occasion came down in Mauretania with a couple of bullets through the wings of her 'plane, which had been fired by nomads. As the letter I have just quoted indicated, she was in a very depressed and miserable state. Already stone-deaf, her eyesight was starting to go, and she was afraid that she might not get her pilot's licence renewed. She still went on with her work at the cottage hospital, getting the best surgeons down from London to assist in the operations and herself doing most of the radiography work. Whenever she was at Woburn she used to go down there quite early in the morning and spend nearly the whole day there.

The hospital was really her main interest in life and the flying exploits merely a side-line. Although her ducal relations had never warmed to her, local people spoke very affectionately and fondly of all her good works. Then my grandfather told her that the expense of the hospital was becoming too much of a drain and that he could no longer afford it. This was a terrible blow to her. It meant the end of the main interest in her life. In a note written not long before she died she said: 'I want a real rest and fresh air and the birds and loneliness.'

She was by now seventy-one years old. On the afternoon of Monday, 22 March, 1937, she took off in her De Havilland Gypsy aeroplane from the hangar at Woburn. The object of the flight was to complete her two hundred hours of solo flying, of which she had already done one hundred and ninety-nine hours and five minutes. Her pilot had suggested to her a course over Buntingford, Girton College and back to Woburn, about eighty-eight miles. She should have been back just within the hour. The weather seemed perfectly favourable at the start although soon clouds closed in and later there was a snowstorm. She was never seen again.

At five o'clock, with dusk falling, the alarm was raised. My grandfather telephoned the Chief Constable of Bedfordshire asking him to take action and an intensive search was carried out over several counties. By the next day a hundred 'planes had joined in the search and all ships at sea were asked to keep a look-out for wreckage. By the twenty-fourth, hope had been given up.

It was not until 2 April that one of the four struts of the 'plane was washed ashore at Yarmouth and positively identified. The three remaining struts came ashore at Gorleston, Lowestoft, and Southwold. Not enough wreckage was ever picked up to ascertain the cause of the accident, if accident it was. I have often wondered whether the combination of failing faculties and her despair over the imminent closure of her beloved hospital did not lead her to seek her end in the one element where she had come to feel at home.

I read in the paper that she was missing, so I hired a car and drove down to Woburn to see my grandfather. It was unheard of, even for members of the family, to visit the house except by pre-arrangement and when the butler opened the door he was horrified and asked whether I had an appointment. I was put into a waiting-room and after half an hour, by which time it was half past twelve, was ushered in to see my grandfather, who was himself eighty years old by then. I said how sorry I was and how anxious he must be and was there anything I could do to help, but he was just as stiff and unbending as ever, even in this moment of family anxiety. In five minutes the interview came to an end. I was not asked to stay to lunch, so I just went straight back to London again. At a time like that it was still impossible, for his own flesh and blood, to get anywhere near him.

CHAPTER FOUR

HENRY VIII SHARES THE SPOILS

I HAD been absolutely fascinated by Woburn, but from the grunts and monosyllables of my grandfather I had prised little enough in the way of details of how it and our other estates had come into the family. Sir Claude Russell was an absolute mine of information, and when he found that I was really interested, would talk for hours about the part the Bedfords have played in English history.

Much nonsense has been written about our origins. One historian, totally misled by a fanciful family tree drawn up for the third Earl of Bedford in 1626, has an ancestor named Hugo de Rosel coming over with William the Conqueror, and traces us back to a lot of Central European Kings with gobbledygook names in medieval times. This record has been put straight by Miss Gladys Scott-Thomson, of Somerville College, Oxford, who in years of devoted work, searching through innumerable outside sources, has produced a series of books on the subject. The trouble with many of the early Russells was that, often with good reason, they destroyed much of their correspondence, and piecing the record together again is not an easy task.

The plain fact is that we are of good lower-middle-class origin, although we did at least start on our way up five hundred years ago. The first Russell in the direct line of which there is indisputable evidence was a Henry Russell, who lived in Dorset and was returned as Burgess for Weymouth in the Parliament of 1425. The family was engaged in the wine trade and had close connexions with Bordeaux, whence their ancestors doubtless came. He made a good marriage, prospered, owned a few parcels of land round Shaftesbury, Stour Provost and Compton Abbas, and in

1440 was appointed the Royal Customs Commissioner for part of Dorset and a couple of Devon ports. It was probably a case of setting a thief to catch a thief. There was a lot of smuggling going on and his prime duty was to see that no wool was exported from the kingdom without paying the necessary fees. Two or three of the sixty-ton barges he used to bring over his wine were impressed into service as coast-guard cutters, of course for a fee.

He was the great-grandfather of the John Russell who became first Earl of Bedford. John was probably born about 1486, and as by the time he died he had acquired not only thousands of acres round Tavistock, but more thousands of acres round Thorney in Cambridgeshire, Covent Garden and Long Acre in London and, by his marriage, the manor of Thornhaugh in Northamptonshire and Chenies in Buckinghamshire—most of the property we have ever owned—he may well be said to be the founder of the family fortunes.

In addition to his undoubted abilities—he was, apart from Cardinal Wolsey, probably the greatest administrator of the reign of Henry VIII—he had the good fortune to grow up in an age when laymen gradually took over the running of the country from the clergy, and rendered his services just at the time when they were rewarded by a share in the abbey and manorial lands which were sequestered and broken up at the Reformation. It was the greatest division of spoils since the Norman Conquest and laid the foundation of the future prosperity of such families as the Russells, the Stanleys, the Cecils and the Petres.

Even so, you have to have luck as well as ability. Young John had spent some time abroad in the family business, and already had fine Italian manners and a remarkable gift of tongues when his great chance came. He was back at home in 1506 when a ship carrying the Archduke Philip of Austria was wrecked at Weymouth. The archduke was escorted to London by a party of Dorset gentlemen, including John Russell, who must on this occasion have met and gained the approval of Henry VII. During the last three years of the King's life he was taken into the household and named a gentleman usher. His long career at Court had begun.

His initial duties were modest enough. The gentlemen ushers had to keep the door of the room in which the King was dining; one of them always had to be in Court by eight in the evening and another had to sit up all night to prevent any unauthorized persons from entering the Great Chamber. One of them attended every day at the solemn function of making the King's bed, ending with the drawing of the curtains and the sprinkling of holy water by an esquire. They were in charge of the pages and lesser functionaries of the Court, organized the great festivities of New Year and Twelfth Night and were responsible for the comfort of all visitors. If an ambassador was of a rank equal to an earl, the ushers had to wait on him themselves, although a yeoman-usher sufficed for anyone of lower rank. They lived in the palace with a carefully regulated allowance of bread, wine and ale for use in their own rooms, as well as candles for lighting and wood for firing, varying according to the time of year.

Henry VII died in 1509 and John quickly attracted the attention of the new young King. For years he was used as a confidential messenger and, I suspect, intelligence agent to the Continent. Serving in the royal garrison at Calais, his wages were eighteen pence a day, with an allowance of four servants, two at eight pence a day and two at six pence. He soon graduated to diplomatic tasks and in 1523 was sent by the King and Cardinal Wolsey as envoy to Charles V. In one of the confused wars of the time, he took part in the Siege of Morlaix in Brittany, for which he was knighted by the Earl of Surrey. It was at this battle that he lost an eye, afterwards his distinguishing mark and clearly shown in the Holbein portrait of him in later years as Lord Privy Seal.

He had already acquired a number of profitable sinecures, including privileged licences for the importation and exportation of wool and wine, but his first properties came from his marriage in 1526 to Anne, the daughter and heiress of

Sir Guy Sapcote, who brought in the Northamptonshire manor of Thornhaugh and the Buckinghamshire estate of Chenies, which for decades was our main family seat and where the family mausoleum of all my ancestors still exists.

In the year of his marriage he was made one of the six gentlemen of the Privy Chamber, two of whom slept each night in the King's bedroom. Eleven years later he was made Comptroller of the Household and then, in 1539, created Baron Russell and a Knight of the Garter. This marked the beginning of his greatest services. To combat the general unrest of the times, a council had been set up for the West Country and Russell was appointed its president, more or less the King's Viceroy, with complete governmental power for the western counties. In order to increase his local standing as a landowner—he had in the meantime disposed of most of the small parcels of land he had inherited —he received from the Crown the dissolved Abbey of St. Mary and St. Rumon in Tavistock. This made his income up to twelve hundred pounds a year, enormous in terms of the times when it is considered that the recently attainted Duke of Buckingham, the greatest landlord in the country, had an income of only just over six thousand pounds. For two years he also held the post of Lord High Admiral and his banner exhibited for the first time the coat of arms which my family still wears.

In common with his contemporaries, he indulged in much land speculation to consolidate his holdings, which I do not need to go into, but it was only on the death of the King he had served so well that he came into the estate now principally identified with the Russell family. Henry VIII had appointed him one of the sixteen counsellors of his infant son, with the promise of an earldom and the wish expressed in his will that he should be granted lands to the value of a hundred pounds a year. At the coronation of Edward VI in February 1547, John Russell was appointed the Great Steward of England.

Shortly thereafter he was granted a reversion of the lease of the Abbey at Woburn, still held by Sir Francis

Bryan, who was steward of the King's manor at Ampthill. The actual value of the Abbey and the grounds was £168 18s. 2d., so that Lord Russell was required to pay the sum of £68 10s. 2d. as annual rent. Three years later he was created the first Earl of Bedford, with fresh grants of land, including manors in Devon and Cornwall belonging to the attainted Marquess of Exeter, more attainted property in Northamptonshire and Bedfordshire and a grant of part of the property that had belonged to Thorney Abbey in Cambridgeshire.

He never lived at Woburn and probably never saw it. It had been a Cistercian abbey which had been seized by the King's commissioners in 1538 at the general dissolution of the monasteries. There were by that time only twelve monks under the abbot and sub-prior, all but one of whom were freed, most of them being given livings or pensions. The abbot, the sub-prior and the twelfth monk were arrested because they had been heard to use treasonable words against the King, particularly the abbot, who had been heard to say: 'It is a marvellous thing that the King's grace could not be contented with that noble Queen, his very true and undoubted wife, Queen Katharine.' All three were tried on the spot, found guilty and hanged, almost certainly on the great oak tree still visible a couple of hundred yards from the west front of the building.

The Covent, or Convent, Garden site and seven acres in Long Acre in London, which my grandfather sold for some two million pounds just before the First World War, came the way of John Russell in 1552, as part of the estates of the attainted Duke of Somerset. Their value at the time was reckoned at £5 3s. 6d. a year.

He lived to a great age for the time and in 1554 went on his last royal mission to Santiago de Compostela in Spain with a retinue of two hundred men to escort King Philip to England to become the husband of Henry VIII's daughter, Mary. Philip was the grandson of the archduke who had been wrecked at Weymouth, thus providing John Russell's first contact with the English Court. He died two years later at the age of seventy. His tomb at Chenies, built of alabaster by Italian workmen, is said to be one of the finest of its kind in Europe.

The first earl, doubtless in a mixture of expediency, personal loyalty and as a means of personal advancement, had followed both his Kings through the religious turmoil of the times. His son Francis, the second earl, was a much more convinced 'reformer' and when Mary was proclaimed Queen in 1553, spent a short period in the Fleet prison. However he fought at his father's side to save Mary's crown in the rebellion of Sir Thomas Wyatt and, on succeeding to the title, was allowed to spend two years in study abroad. In Zürich he came under the influence of the Swiss church reformers, strengthening his Puritan turn of mind, which he transmitted to all the Bedfords active in the sixteenth and seventeenth centuries. He had inherited his father's gift of languages and diplomatic ability, and was as great a servant of Queen Elizabeth as his father had been to her father and half-brother. Among his many claims to fame, he was a god-father to Sir Francis Drake. He was also the first Russell to adopt the motto *Che sara sara*—What will be will be—which remains the family motto to this day.

He died in 1585 with a considerable load of debt. Five years earlier he had petitioned the Queen declaring that his embassy to France, his attendance at the christening of the young Prince James at Stirling, his duties as a Privy Counsellor and his work as a Lieutenant of the three western counties had been accompanied by no money allowance. There were arrears of payments due to the Crown and borrowings amounting to nearly nine thousand pounds. A nobleman's funeral in those days was a very lavish affair and had to be paid for in cash, so the contents of the house at Chenies and part of the furniture at Bedford House in the Strand had to be sold to meet the immediate expenses of some two thousand pounds.

The situation was not helped by his complicated succession. The three eldest sons had all predeceased him. His grandson, Edward, became the third earl as a minor.

He was a weak-willed spendthrift who died without issue and almost wrecked the estate for good. As a young man he became embroiled in the Essex rebellion, only escaping with his head by paying a heavy fine. His wife, the former Lucy Harington, friend of poets and painters and a great favourite at Court, was much better at spending money than she was at saving it. However, our family and the world owe her one great debt of gratitude. The famous Armada portrait of Queen Elizabeth, a Gheeraerts studio piece, was almost certainly acquired by her. It hangs in Woburn to this day, one of our most prized possessions.

Countess Lucy described herself as 'a very diligent gatherer of all I can get of Holbein's or any other excellent master's hand', and she is responsible for several of the older canvases still in the possession of the family. A few must have come down from the first and second earls, particularly the portraits of such contemporaries and friends as the Cecil family and the Earls of Courtenay and Essex. The picture of Mary Tudor by Il Moro, together with Hans Eworth's painting of her sitting with Philip of Spain in the state room at Whitehall, were probably presented to the first earl in recognition of his services in escorting her husband to England.

To meet some of his debts, the third earl considered selling Woburn and the Covent Garden estate. The family patrimony was only saved by the cadet branch which had become the presumptive heir. The third earl's surviving uncle, William Russell, youngest son of the second earl, had inherited his full share of the family's administrative ability. He had become a lieutenant-general of cavalry and in 1586 took part in the Battle of Zutphen. It was to him that the dying Sir Philip Sidney bequeathed his best gilt armour as a token of friendship. William Russell became Governor of Flushing, Lord Deputy of Ireland, and in 1603 was created Baron Russell of Thornhaugh by James I. He took his title from the share of the family estate left to him by his father, which also included the thousands of acres of Thorney Abbey in Cambridgeshire.

He was also the Russell who started the preliminary work on the tremendous project of draining the fens, which came to be known as the Bedford Level. While Governor of Flushing he had been very much impressed by the dyke building and land reclamation activities of the Dutch and brought three experts over to Cambridgeshire to report on the possibility of using the same methods in England. The Privy Council granted permission to carry out various drainage schemes, but the main part of the work was put in hand by his son, Francis, who, on the death of his cousin Edward in 1627, became the fourth Earl of Bedford.

The fourth earl was the first Russell to make a home out of Woburn. For the best part of three-quarters of a century the old Abbey had lain more or less derelict, but its resuscitation was largely a matter of chance and the uneasy relationship between the third earl and his cousin. Edward had been prevented from selling any part of the Bedford estate when Francis, the heir, petitioned the King not to permit the alienation of any part of it. He was living at the time in Chiswick, and when a bad epidemic of the plague broke out in London in 1625, he managed to persuade his cousin to allow him and his family of ten children to go and live at Woburn to escape its ravages. Two years later he succeeded to the title.

This fourth earl was a fine figure of a man and there is a magnificent portrait of him at Woburn by Van Dyck, showing him in the severe black habit and plain, broad white collar of his Puritan persuasions. A thrifty and influential man, he not only succeeded in putting the family finances in order, but became a patron of Inigo Jones, the great architect. Their most profitable venture together was the building of the Piazza on the Covent Garden estate. London was expanding fast and the magnificent colonnaded houses were soon let to wealthy members of the aristocracy and the new merchant class looking for a fashionable place to live. Part of the development included the architect's masterpiece of St. Paul's Church, still a Covent Garden landmark.

They then turned their attention to Woburn. It is not quite certain to what extent Inigo Jones was responsible for the whole rebuilding plan, but he certainly acted as an adviser. Most of the old Abbey was torn down and little was left except the stones used for the foundations of the new house, which was built around a square court-yard, with gabled wings, high-pitched roofs, stone finials and grouped chimneys. According to the Italian taste of the time, ludicrously unsuitable to the British climate, the sun was avoided and the principal living-rooms and family bedrooms placed in the north wing, which still survives to-day after the second reconstruction more than a hundred years later.

On the ground floor, originally intended as a sitting-out place for the family, opening on to the garden through a three-arched loggia, was that odd fancy which has also survived the centuries, the grotto, a vaulted cave decorated with ormer shells, elaborate stone figures and stalagmites, and a wall fountain. There were some ninety rooms in the Inigo Jones house, including eleven sitting-rooms. Among the paintings they hung in them were those of the seven eldest sons and daughters, made by the Hungarian portraitest Priwitzer, in which young Lord William Russell, the second son, aged fourteen at the time, was shown in the sweeping pink robes of the Order of the Bath, an honour bestowed on him at the coronation of Charles I.

Meanwhile, work on the Bedford Level proceeded apace, absorbing every spare penny of revenue from the estate and involving it in a certain amount of debt again. It was certainly a major project. The fourth earl and his associates were to receive 95,000 acres of land, of which 12,000 were to be set apart for the King and the profits of 40,000 reserved as security for keeping up the drainage works. By the time he died, Earl Francis had spent more than a hundred thousand pounds on the undertaking. A number of Dutch and French refugees from religious persecution were settled there and were the first people to introduce the cultivation of the colza cabbage, which provided a cheap and popular source of oil for lamps.

In politics he was an associate of Pym, and in 1640 he was the ring-leader of the twelve peers who urged King Charles to call a Parliament and make peace with the Scots. He was regarded as one of the people best qualified to act as a mediator between the King and the Popular Party, and the subsequent history of the Stuarts might well have been different if he had not fallen ill of the small-pox and died the following year, on the morning of the day when Charles gave his assent to the Bill of Attainder on Strafford. During his life he had written ten folio volumes, still in the study at Woburn to-day, on the subject of religious doctrine and dogma. I am not at all sure that my own father did not derive some inspiration from this example.

Francis, the heir, had died only a month before his father and it was the second son, William, who became the fifth earl. The third son, John, did not share his father's politics, and became a colonel in the Royalist Army and was an active Royalist conspirator during the Protectorate period. Later, in 1660, he raised and for twenty-one years commanded Charles II's Regiment of Foot Guards, now the Grenadier Guards.

The fifth earl lived through five reigns and Cromwell's Protectorate, dying in the first year of the eighteenth century at the age of eighty-seven. As he provided the family with its dukedom, and set up a pattern of somewhat withdrawn residence at Woburn, followed in the main by all but one of his successors, he merits more detailed study. Both factors came about more or less by accident, as a result of the troubled history of the times. The dukedom was granted by William and Mary as a sop for the execution of his son by Charles II and the long residence at Woburn was more the result of prudence than anything else.

His marriage had provided a welcome touch of romance. Among his parents' neighbours at Chiswick had been Robert Carr, Earl of Somerset, at one time a favourite of James I. His wife, Frances Howard, the former Countess of Essex, had been found guilty of poisoning Sir Thomas Overbury in one of the most sensational trials in history, and husband and wife had been committed to the Tower, where the countess gave birth to a child, Lady Anne Carr. When she grew up young William Russell fell in love with her. His father, who had heard the countess's confession at her trial in the House of Lords, was horrified and refused his consent. However, Charles I took the young man's side and on a visit to Woburn Abbey in July 1636, the King and Henrietta Maria persuaded the father to change his mind, although the marriage did not take place for another year, when Anne had a full-length portrait painted by Van Dyck, perhaps the loveliest picture we have at Woburn. Van Dyck had also painted a portrait of William in company with his friend George, Lord Digby, who, as Earl of Bristol, became his brother-in-law. However, this is now at Althorp in the possession of the Spencer family. There is an eighteenth-century copy made by Knapton at Woburn. William's marriage was an extraordinarily happy one, although his father-in-law defaulted on his daughter's dowry. However, this deficiency was more than made up by his son and grandson, both of whom married great heiresses.

The fifth earl soon found himself caught up in the conflict between King and Parliament, in which he played a some-what equivocal part. In 1642 Parliament appointed him Lord-Lieutenant of the Counties of Devon and Somerset and made him a general-of-horse in the Parliamentary Army. He besieged the Marquess of Hertford in Sherborne Castle and then in October his silver banner, diapered with black and fringed with black and silver, was carried before him at the Battle of Edge Hill. The captain of the 67th Troop of Horse under his command was Oliver Cromwell.

However, Bedford tried to steer a middle course between the forces of the Stuarts and Parliament and severed his connexion with the Parliamentary Party before the end of the year. With Lord Holland and Lord Clare, he visited the King at Oxford and Gloucester to offer their services. After the failure of the peace proposals put forward in the House of Lords in August 1643, Bedford switched frankly to the royal cause and fought for the King at the Siege of Gloucester and the first Battle of Newbury. Then he changed sides again, probably not uninfluenced by the fact that Parliamentary commissioners had levied a fine of eight hundred pounds, and carried off from Bedford House in the Strand most of its furniture and valuable tapestries to meet the assessment.

The fifth earl made his peace with the Parliamentary forces and surrendered himself to the Earl of Essex at the end of December 1643. From then until the Restoration he took little part in English politics and concentrated on the administration of his estates, including the successful completion of the drainage works on the Bedford Level started by his grandfather. However, the King did stay briefly at Woburn in 1645, and it was there, in July 1647, that the Army presented to him the document known as The Heads of the Proposals, as a basis for negotiations, which the King rejected, thus making his execution inevitable.

We know quite a lot about the way the fifth earl lived. All his household account-books have survived. The accounting system was primitive enough. When he inherited the title, the dowager countess formally handed over to him the keys of the great chest, which stood in Bedford House and served as the family bank. The chest is now at Woburn. It was probably made in the Netherlands for his grandfather, as the exterior is painted in characteristic Dutch fashion, the squares showing prim landscapes, with flowers, roses and tulips. The spring of the great double lock which fits the whole of the lid is Spanish in style. When he took it over it contained exactly £1,557 14s. 1d. Into it over the years went the rents collected from his various estates. His income between 5 July 1641, and the same day the following year, was just under £8,500.

This was soon augmented, as during the sixteen-forties and -fifties the Covent Garden Piazza became the fashionable place to live. The rent roll included a number of titled

85

people, such as the Marquess of Winchester and the Earl of Sussex, and soon went up to £1,500 a year. At one point, when the Parliamentary commissioners tried to make a valuation of the property with a view to levying a tax on the capital, the earl managed to avoid it by pointing out that his father had spent £4,886 building St. Paul's Church and that this ought to be taken into account. It was not until after the Restoration that he obtained a royal licence to hold a market within the Covent Garden Piazza. By the end of the sixteen-fifties the estate was more or less clear of the debts which had been caused by his father borrowing money for the Bedford Level project, and by the necessity of finding dowries for his sisters.

One of the Covent Garden tenants was Peter Lely, the painter, whose portrait of two of the little daughters, Anne and Diana, we still have. It depicts them in a garden, with Anne helping herself to the red cherries which her sister holds in her skirt, with a little negro servant by their side holding a basket of roses. Very soon after it was finished Anne died after eating poisonous berries in the garden. There are also two Lely portraits of the fifth earl, one showing him three-quarter length, dressed in one of his Indian gowns, a loose flowing robe of figured silk, a form of dress of which he was very fond. This painting went out of the family, but was bought back in the twentieth century. However, the other showing him full length in his robes as Knight of the Garter, has always remained at Woburn.

His household consisted of a receiver-general who had a salary of a hundred pounds a year, and was a sort of general manager of all the properties; under him there was a principal clerk and a retained auditor and lawyer. John Thornton, a famous Nonconformist divine, was the tutor with a salary of thirty pounds a year, and remained with the family all his life. The gentleman of the privy purse had a salary of twenty pounds a year; there was a chaplain, a steward with forty pounds a year and a house bailiff, his assistant, with twenty pounds a year. The dozen or so footmen were paid between two pounds and six pounds with their keep, and the pages were clothed and fed, but paid nothing.

At Woburn the earl reserved for his own use only the gardens and well-wooded deer park. Otherwise it was divided into tenant holdings and there was nothing in the nature of a home farm. Most of the food came from Thorney Abbey, which the earl rebuilt as it stands to-day, chiefly for the occupation of his agent, Mr. George Collop. This provided most of the meat and venison, with the cattle driven across country from Cambridgeshire for killing. Feathered game came from the Chenies estate and most of the fish they ate was fresh-water fish, pike and perch, which came from his own ponds at Woburn.

Quite a lot of food was bought on the open market, although for a large household the bills were modest enough. Oysters, straight from Colchester, cost two shillings a barrel, beef cost up to two shillings a stone, and mutton up to half a crown. A calf's head was eightpence or ninepence. Coffee was about five shillings a pound, but tea was very expensive, twenty-five shillings a pound, and later, when the duty rose, as much as three guineas a pound. Wine was imported principally in barrel, and the pleasures of champagne and vintage wine imported in bottle only became available after the Restoration. The earl had his own wine import licence, for which he paid twenty-four shillings. Four dozen bottles of what was probably Châteauneuf du Pape cost sixty-two shillings, two hogsheads of port wine ten pounds and the usual price for Canary wine was seven shillings a gallon.

Visits to the Tavistock estate in the West were infrequent, but the earl and countess rode quite often to Thorney to watch the final progress of the drainage works, and sometimes went to Cambridge, where he had special connexions with Trinity College. Some of the splendid dinners he gave at the Red Lion Hotel there used to cost him as much as fifteen pounds. The earl rode in state everywhere with his own band, his coming heralded by the sound of harps, trumpets and bells. His chief pleasure was hunting, which in his case meant hunting by hawk. His falconer was one of the highest paid men on the establishment and received a hundred pounds a year.

In 1660 the earl and his second son, William, dressed in their finest satins and brocades, were two of the peers who rode in the procession to welcome Charles II. The month after the accession the earl paid £43 12s. 6d. for a letter patent of pardon absolving him from anything he might have done contrary to His Majesty during the King's absence from the country.

Francis, the eldest son, had always been a sickly child. He spent his life touring England and the Continent with a tutor in search of the health that he never found. He predeceased his father by many years and William became the heir. William was a brilliant man, one of the outstanding figures of his age, and he made a fitting marriage. His wife was Rachel, one of the three daughters and co-heiress of Thomas Wriothesley, fourth Earl of Southampton, whose father had been the patron of Shakespeare. His estate was divided by lot, and Rachel's part was the manor of Blooms-bury and St. Giles, with Southampton House and an estate in Hampshire. It was considered at the time that she had got the worst of the bargain, but as we are still living pre-cariously off the proceeds of the Bloomsbury estate to-day, I have no cause for complaint.

Southampton himself had developed the area just south of his house as a miniature housing estate. The 146 tenants accounted for a rent roll of just over twelve hundred pounds, while the fields and meadows to the north were let out for farming purposes and brought in just under four hundred pounds a year. Perhaps I ought to mention as a footnote that Rachel's half-sister, Elizabeth, married the Earl of Montagu. They built themselves a house on the plot just to the west of Southampton House, which, nearly a century later, was bought by the nation for use as the 'general repository' to be known as the British Museum.

Lord William Russell came to a violent end. Brought up in the anti-papist tradition by his friend and tutor, John Thornton, his opinions were strengthened by his wife, who had Huguenot blood on her mother's side. Southampton House and Montagu House became the headquarters of a political party, the members of which may fairly be called the early Whigs. From 1679 onwards, William Russell took an active part in the religious turmoil into which England was plunged. Charles II was suspected of turning towards the Church of Rome and his brother and heir, James, Duke of York, was assumed to be a Roman Catholic. In the House of Commons William Russell demanded the removal of James from the King's Council. In 1680 he was among those who entered Westminster Hall to present James to the Grand Jury as a popish recusant, although the matter never came to trial. Later in the year he was the leader of the group which included the Lord Mayor and aldermen of the City of London who presented the second Exclusion Bill in Parliament.

Then he was implicated in the Rye House Plot. In 1683 an informant told the government that it was intended to assassinate the King and James as they rode past Rye House on their way from Newmarket to Westminster. Whether William Russell was an active plotter, or merely knew of their intentions, was never conclusively proved, but he was arrested and brought to trial, with Rachel sitting below him in court to take notes for his defence—a famous incident, although the picture we have at Woburn portraying it was painted very much later. Holding steadfastly to the opinion that a subject may under certain conditions resist the sovereign, he was sentenced to death. Rachel brought their three children, two little girls and a boy of three, to Newgate to bid their father farewell. Later the same evening she went back herself, when Bishop Burnet, who had attended William throughout the trial, was present. They listened to his last sermon together and afterwards the manuscript was handed to Rachel, together with the speech William intended to make the following dawn on the scaffold. These manuscripts, together with the text of the main speech he made at the trial, are still at Woburn, the writing as fresh and clear as when they were first penned.

He was executed at Lincoln's Inn Fields on 21 July. It is said that James, Duke of York, wanted the execution to be carried out in front of Southampton House as a warning to all noble traitors. The newly formed regiments of the King's Horse and Foot kept a cordon round him and although he was not able to deliver his final speech, it was quickly printed as a broadsheet and sold in the London streets. The severed head was bound to the body again and his remains rest with all the other Russells at Chenies. Ever after, Rachel kept Friday, the last day she had seen her husband, as a day of meditation and self-examination. No visitor might be received at Southampton House or at any other house she owned. In letters which we still have, she told her children to keep three days of mourning: 26 June, the day of her husband's arrest, 3 July, the day when he was brought to trial, and 21 July, the day of his execution. The earl, broken-hearted, had addressed a petition to the King and is said to have offered fifty thousand pounds for a pardon, but it was all in vain.

After the execution, the old earl was worried that the estates and title might be forfeited by the heir, his grandson. He took learned legal advice and all the opinions agreed that neither the estates nor the title could be forfeited since the attainted man had never possessed either, and that his son was therefore the natural heir of his grandfather. With the accession of William and Mary, their first Parliament passed an Act which reversed the attainder of William Lord Russell, declaring the condemnation to be null and void. This declaration was made by letters patent handed to the earl in April 1689, a document we still possess. The Act also contained an injunction that all the proceedings relative to the trial and execution should be 'wholly cancelled and taken off the file and otherwise defaced and obliterated'. This was actually done and there is no trace of the matter in official records whatsoever.

In 1694 the fifth earl was created Duke of Bedford and Marquess of Tavistock. The preamble stated specifically that he had received this step in the peerage by reason 'that he was the father to the Lord Russell, the ornament of his age, whose great merit it was not enough to transmit by history to posterity'. The various fees and duties involved in the promotion cost the old duke £1,204 11s. 9d.

Shortly after their father's death, the earl's three grand-children were painted by Sir Godfrey Kneller. The two little girls are aged about twelve and nine, and little Wrio-thesley about five, dressed according to the fashion of the day in an antique Roman military costume of lilac and green over a blue cuirass. Young Wriothesley made the most remarkable marriage of all the Russells. In 1695, at the age of fourteen and a half, he was married to a girl of thirteen. Her name was Elizabeth Howland. She came of a family of merchants, so the idea of people with titles marrying rich heiresses is by no means such a new one. The family first appears in the reign of Elizabeth, when Giles Howland prospered sufficiently as a draper in the City to buy the manor of Tooting Bec, which included the village of Streatham. Throughout the seventeenth century the family grew rich, and his son John Howland became Sheriff of Surrey. His son, another John, made in 1681 a very wealthy match with Elizabeth, one of the daughters of Sir Josiah Child, head of the East India Company. Elizabeth was their only child and she brought to the marriage a dowry of a hundred thousand pounds. In order to preserve the name, the Barony of Howland was created for the Russell family, which is how I came by the title I bore all the time my grandfather was alive.

After the wedding, the young pair only met at intervals for some years. The young bride remained with her mother, and the groom was sent abroad with a tutor. Apparently her mother got on splendidly with the old duke, who started to take up shares in the ships of the East India Company. He found it an excellent way of importing goods for himself and many of the fine pieces of oriental china at Woburn date from this time. He brought tea tables from India and several sets of teapots and cups from China. He was also associated with this astute business-woman in planning and carrying through the building of a dry dock and then of the wet dock at Rotherhithe.

This was not the only maritime connexion the old duke had. Edward Russell, the son of his younger brother, became one of the naval heroes of the time. He was a regular officer, but seems to have resigned his command on the execution of his cousin William. He became an active agent of William of Orange in England and during the reign of James II made several journeys to Holland in the prince's interest. As a reward, he was appointed in 1689 a treasurer of the navy. However, his political allegiances seem to have been as fickle as his uncle's, as by 1691 he was in correspondence with the exiled James again, and apparently ready to act as much as a traitor to King William as he had to his predecessor. In the year 1692 he found himself as Admiral of the Blue in command of eighty-two British and Dutch ships with little option but to engage the French fleet which had just left Brest. After a confused action in which the French were scattered, a proportion of them was driven westwards towards Cap La Hogue, where, in the bay, twelve ships of the line and eight transports were burnt. It was considered a great victory and Edward Russell became subsequently, on three occasions, First Lord of the Admiralty.

The young Marquess of Tavistock had graduated from Magdalen and then went on a long tour abroad, where he spent a lot of time in Rome and got into bad gambling habits. At one time he had to borrow nearly three thousand pounds on which interest had to be paid up to the day of his death. He arrived back in England just in time to see his grandfather in the last year of his life. The old man was now nearly blind—bad eyesight has been a recurrent failing in our family—and his account-books were full of entries for the purchase of glasses, which he was always breaking, and gallons of eye lotion. He died on 27 September 1700, at the age of eighty-seven at Bedford House in the Strand.

CHAPTER FIVE

DUKES MERRY AND OTHERWISE

RACHEL, the forcibly widowed mother of the second duke, came out of her retirement to make sure that her son received all the honours which should have accrued to his father. Even before the old duke had been laid to rest at Chenies, she had written a somewhat oblique letter to King William asking what should be done with his Garter insignia and robes. She took advantage of the somewhat evasive reply to retain them in the family, contrary to all usage. Young Wriothesley was also created a Knight of the Garter, his companion at the ceremony, also just appointed, being John Churchill, who became Duke of Marlborough the same year. As a further sign of royal favour, Rachel also asked that the family whose heir her daughter had married, the Earl and Countess of Rutland, should have a dukedom conferred on them. This also was done, and at the coronation of Queen Anne in 1702, the young Duke of Bedford was chosen to perform the office of Lord High Constable. No one could have asked for more complete rehabilitation.

Wriothesley was a very fortunate young man. Just after he came of age he drew up a statement of his income, which showed a total of £22,271 17s. 9½d., of which three thousand pounds still went to his mother, and three thousand pounds was settled on his wife. The careful administration of the old duke had paid handsome fruit and the estate itself stood clear and unencumbered of all but the gambling debt. Part of the Devon properties round Tavistock had been sold off, but the value of both Covent Garden and Thorney had risen enormously. He consolidated further by pulling down the old Bedford House in the Strand, and the young couple shared Southampton House with his mother, an arrangement which apparently worked very well, although the duke and duchess could always escape to Woburn or the house of her own family at Streatham. They also retained the residence still known as Bedford House on Chiswick Mall. This went out of the family and I tried, unsuccessfully, to buy it back nearly two hundred and fifty years later.

During his brief life, Wriothesley became known as a patron of the arts, almost the only one we have had in the family. The only tune his old grandfather was ever known to have approved was a local melody called 'The Woburn Tune', otherwise entitled 'The Four-and-Twenty Fiddlers'. However, his grandson, largely as a result of his prolonged Italian tour, had two Italian musicians, Niccolo Cosimi and Niccolo Francesco Haym, attached to his household. He also built up quite a large collection of paintings and prints, valuable books and editions of music. Some of these are still at Woburn, but most of them were dispersed by subsequent dukes.

His career was cut short in 1711, soon after the birth of their youngest child, when in spite of the warnings of their physician, Dr. Hans Sloane, who considered it a danger area, the family went to spend a period at Streatham, where he caught small-pox and died. He left two daughters, a son aged three, another Wriothesley, and the infant, John. They were brought up by their mother and grandmother. Rachel lived for another twelve years and only died in 1723 at the age of eighty-seven. Born in 1636, when Charles I reigned before the Civil War, she had lived into the tenth year of George I. The following year, Elizabeth the duchess died, also of small-pox, at Streatham. Of her two daughters, Rachel had married Scroop, the Duke of Bridgwater, a widower with a young daughter, Anne, whose mother had been a daughter of John Churchill, Duke of Marlborough and his wife, Sarah.

The young third duke married his sister's stepdaughter. His brother, Lord John Russell, in due course married Lady Diana Spencer, daughter of the third Earl of Sunderland, who had also married a daughter of the Duchess of Marlborough. Both the brothers therefore had the redoubtable Sarah as a grandmother-in-law. It was to be an uneasy relationship.

The third duke was a wastrel and a gambler, and if he had not obliged us all by dying young, there would not be much of a story left for me to tell. Income from the estate was expanding all the time. The square to the south of Southampton House was now generally referred to as Bloomsbury Square and the whole stretch from King Street to Tottenham Court Road was now becoming quite closely built up, although the gardens to the north were still open, and there was nothing beyond them until you got to Hampstead and Highgate. By 1732 the area from Great Russell Street to the Holborn High Road was filled with houses, and the rent roll had increased to three thousand, seven hundred pounds, double what it had been when the second duke took over in 1700. Nevertheless his son got through enormous sums of money, and was not only thinking of cutting down all the timber in Woburn Park, but actually of selling the Bloomsbury estate he had inherited from his mother.

He was much harried by his termagant grandmother-in-law. She used to tell him that Woburn was tumbling round about his ears, to which he replied that it would last his time, as if he had a premonition of his early death. Sarah used to tell her contemporaries that he was treating his wife badly, and called him a brute. However, she had by now also fallen out of sympathy with her granddaughter, whose portrait at Blenheim was seen one day to be covered with black paint, and underneath in Sarah's own hand the sinister remark, 'But she is much blacker inside.'

The crusty old lady has left a description of a visit she paid to Woburn in July 1732, when she was in her seventy-third year. She was carried round the house in a sedan chair, but her young host, aged twenty-four, annoyed her by dropping into a convenient seat each time they made a halt, which may account for her verdict that she thought less than nothing of the portraits. The gallery indeed contained, as she wrote to another granddaughter, a great many pictures, but their only value as far as she herself could discern was that they belonged to the family and were in antique dresses. So much for Van Dyck, although she commented approvingly on his portrait of Anne Carr. However, she liked the layout of the house, and two ceilings in the north wing particularly caught her eye: 'I think them very pretty because they are not done as they do them now, but the work is not more raised than my Lady De La Warr would make an embroidered mantua. . . . The pattern is very small and pretty.' They are still there and my visitors can see them for half a crown.

Later in the same year the health of the third duke finally collapsed, and he was ordered to take a voyage to Lisbon to see if this would cure him. 'If the Duke of Bedford escapes being sick at sea,' his grandmother commented callously to her other granddaughter, Diana, 'I fancy he may get to Lisbon. But if he should not, I think I told you that Doctor Meade was of opinion that it would kill him.' She was quite right. Wriothesley's dead body was put ashore at Corunna.

His brother, Lord John, now the fourth duke, and his wife started off on a much better footing with Sarah. Diana had always been her favourite granddaughter, and to the end she lavished all her affection on her. As soon as they succeeded, she commissioned a fashionable, albeit second-rate artist named Isaac Whood to make portraits of the fourth duke and duchess and to copy portraits of herself and the first Duke of Marlborough. These were exchanged and the Marlborough portraits are still at Woburn.

However, in 1735 the young duchess died of consumption at the age of twenty-five and, after two years of widowerhood, the duke married again. His bride was Gertrude Leveson-Gower, daughter of the first Earl Gower. Sarah thought little of this move and just before his remarriage engaged in an acrimonious correspondence with her former grandson-in-law. She wanted him to return a tent belonging to the first Duke of Marlborough which she had lent to her granddaughter to sit in as her illness got worse. She also accused the duke of trying to keep for himself all the jewels which she had given or lent to her granddaughter at her wedding.

As a parting shot she said that she was no longer going to leave him the hundred thousand pounds she had promised Diana in her will, and ended her last letter with a classic piece of invective:

> I am so sincere, that I will end with saying that I wish I could with truth profess I had any respect for you: which I do not think anybody that reads this account can really have, since there is not one tittle aggravated but a great many things omitted of the same nature, to save tediousness, and therefore, I am sure Your Grace in your own mind will excuse me for saying no more than that I am Your Grace's most humble servant, Sarah Marlborough.

At least the fourth duke had learnt better than his brother the thrifty habits, mind for business and orderly keeping of accounts instilled into him by his Howland mother. Over the years he kept the estate intact and in the end made it solvent again. Not that this made him in any way dull. Horace Walpole calls him the 'merry little Duke'. He was very active politically, and as an anti-Walpole Whig was the leader of the group of politicians generally known as the Bloomsbury Group, or by their opponents the Bloomsbury Gang. During Bonnie Prince Charlie's rebellion of 1745 he raised a regiment of foot for the King, was appointed its colonel, and marched north with it. He would have commanded it in person if he had not been prevented by a bad attack of the gout from which he suffered all his life. On his recovery he found it at Edinburgh after the battle of Culloden.

He held many high offices. He was successively First Lord of the Admiralty, Principal Secretary of State, Lord-Lieutenant for Ireland and Ambassador to France. The

Duke of Newcastle was jealous of him, and his brother, Pelham, the First Minister, complained of his idleness, saying that with him it was 'all jollity, boyishness and vanity', and that he was almost always at Woburn. Horace Walpole says that he seemed to care more for sport, and especially for cricket, than for politics and although that may be true he certainly lived a busy public life. He was a successful Lord-Lieutenant of Ireland and did much to reconcile Catholic opinion, although in the end it led nowhere. He was also a friend and patron of James Wolfe, the victor at Quebec.

It was not until fifteen years after he had succeeded to the title that the duke considered his finances were in sufficiently good order to do something about the now thoroughly decrepit house at Woburn. It was just about the same time when William Bentinck, the second Duke of Portland, was rebuilding Welbeck and the Duke of Devonshire was re-building Chatsworth. In 1747, Duke John invited the architect Henry Flitcroft to pay a visit to Woburn. He was at that time master carpenter of the Board of Works and known to his contemporaries as 'Burlington Harry', from his first patron, the architecturally-minded Lord Burlington, who had originally noted his talent.

Flitcroft was instructed to retain the north wing with its grotto and part of the west wing, but the rest of the house was in such poor condition that it had to be knocked down and completely rebuilt. The old rooms were all refurbished and it is fascinating to note from the accounts that the men employed to clean the corridor out of which those on the ground floor opened, referred to it as Paternoster Row, which is the name by which it would have been known in the old Abbey, two and a half centuries earlier.

Flitcroft's innovations included the installation of a bath with running hot water and—probably the first one on historical record—a water-closet, which was built in the north garden and specifically reserved for the use of his grace. One result of this was that the water supply ran short, in spite of constructing reservoirs and a system of pipes. This remained a problem for years to come. Flitcroft imported earthenware stoves from France to warm the passages and staircases and also hung a great chandelier, the first to appear at Woburn, in the main saloon, where it is still to-day. The duke had continued the family interest in the East India Company and through them imported the Chinese wallpaper which was put up in two of the bedrooms in the north wing. Its total cost was sixteen pounds, seven shillings and it is still there.

Flitcroft also acted as the duke's adviser for his Bloomsbury property, and was probably responsible for the first development at its northern end. A new road was being cut from the Edgware Road near Paddington to Islington, passing to the north of the Duke of Bedford's fields, through land owned by the Duke of Grafton. The fourth duke therefore had a new private road built running north between his property and the new road, and he was responsible for the project of building a new square, modelled on the King's Circus at Bath, at the northern end of his Bloomsbury fields. It was only completed after his death but it still forms what is known as Bedford Square. Southampton House, which he had renamed Bedford House, also had in its large dining-room at this time eight views of Venice painted by Canaletto, while in the adjacent small eating-room there were sixteen others. Later these were all taken to Woburn, where we also have them in the dining-room, although there is no indication of how they actually came into the family.

The fourth duke sent his son Francis to school, something which seems to happen in the Bedford family about once a century. The young Marquess of Tavistock attended Westminster School, where the two younger sons of the first duke had gone in the year of the Restoration. The fee for his board was twenty-five pounds a year, ten pounds was paid for his room, and another five pounds for a fire.

The pattern of the household economy had changed very little since the first duke's lifetime, although beer had become a much more staple drink and was always served at breakfast. Much more tea was being drunk and, for the first time, milk was being added. Silver teapots and little milk jugs started to put in their appearance. The senior official, a Mr. Butcher, was now called his agent-in-chief and received a salary of seven hundred pounds a year, although he lived in a house of his own and had to pay all his own expenses. In 1756 Butcher had all the estate deeds and accounts running back through the centuries sorted, filed and endorsed, and it is due to him that the household accounts of the family have been preserved although, as I have said, very little in the way of letters and correspondence has survived.

The other household wages had remained about the same. His principal cook was a Frenchman, who got sixty pounds a year, with an English cook who received thirty pounds, and a confectioner who received fifty-two pounds, ten shillings a year. Four or five kitchen-maids had ousted the men and boys of the earlier century and they got eight pounds a year, while the confectioner's maid got only five pounds. With the butler, under-butler and groom-of-the-chambers, there were still ten footmen, who in the seventeen-fifties were receiving between six pounds and eight pounds yearly, although twenty years later their wages had been increased to between fourteen and seventeen pounds a year.

Travelling conditions had improved. It took Rachel and William Russell in their heavy coach between twelve and sixteen hours to travel between Woburn and Great Russell Street, a distance of forty-two miles, and very often they stayed the night at St. Albans or Dunstable. The fourth duke used the lighter post-chaise and, with the improvement of the roads under the turnpike trust, probably took about four hours for the journey. The heavier coaches were kept at Woburn and the post-chaises at Bedford House, doubtless the beginning of the system still maintained by my grandfather.

During the early part of the fourth duke's life his agents and factors were making their purchases for the household in the City, St. Paul's Churchyard and Ludgate Hill, with some of the vegetables coming from Covent Garden. The best shops were springing up in the neighbourhood of St. James's Square and Piccadilly. They still bought wax candles for Bedford House from Hannah Jones in the Poultry, who sent forty-eight pounds of white wax lights every month at the price of two and tenpence a pound. Samuel Strode, the oil and colour man, lived near by, and sold them vast quantities of lamp oil weekly at the price of two and fourpence a gallon.

Men's fashions were changing. Coats and breeches were starting to be made out of fine cloth rather than silk, satin, brocade or velvet, which were now used chiefly for their very richly ornamented waistcoats. The fourth duke must have been something of a dandy, and was always buying rich and expensive cloths from a woollen draper named Gabriel Fouace at the Pearl and Crown in Bedford Street, Covent Garden. He was often paying up to twenty-five shillings a yard for superfine cloth. The orange livery cloth for his menservants, which was bought in lots of sixty or seventy yards at a time, cost ten shillings a yard, while orange, yellow or brown shalloon, which was probably for the lining, cost one and eightpence a yard. The men's overcoats were made out of kersey, a coarse narrow cloth, supplied in lengths of sixty or more yards at a time at a cost of six shillings a yard.

In his various official positions he wore particularly sumptuous clothes. One of Gainsborough's best portraits shows him wearing a coat of scarlet cloth. In a painting by Sir Joshua Reynolds—both of them are at Woburn—he wears his peer's robes with a gala coat of blue velvet. Another portrait now in the residence of the Provost of Trinity College, Dublin, shows him wearing a green satin coat in his capacity as Lord-Lieutenant of Ireland, and Chancellor of the University of Dublin.

One of the most fascinating relics is a bill for a blue and white habit for one of his daughters, Lady Caroline Russell. The duchess must have had a similar outfit, as an anecdote is recounted of when Admiral of the Fleet, the Honourable

John Forbes, had been called in by George II to discuss a design for a naval uniform. He suggested a mixture of red and blue as being the national colours. The duke told him of the king's decision: 'The King is determined otherwise, for having seen my Duchess riding in the park a few days ago in a habit of blue faced with white, the dress took the fancy of His Majesty, who has appointed it for the uniform of the Royal Navy.'

An interesting, and I must say eminently practical, habit they had in those days, was to borrow glass, china and plate from their friends for special occasions. For instance, for a ball in May of 1757 at Bedford House, the plate was borrowed from the Duke of Marlborough, Lord Bolingbroke, Lord Gower, Lady Ossory and Lady Betty Waldegrave. It used to be carried to and fro by chairmen, each of whom received a tip for the service. They even used to borrow each other's footmen, each of whom was paid a guinea a night for his help.

The fourth duke himself wrote of his 'inveterate habit of destroying all personal correspondence'. This included letters written to him, as well as the copies of those he wrote himself. In the following century, his great-grandson, Lord John Russell, the Victorian statesman, edited such political correspondence of his predecessor as had been allowed to survive, but he eliminated and, I fear, destroyed finally all papers which did not appear to him of sufficient importance, by which he apparently meant those which did not have to do with political affairs. Only two or three personal letters have escaped this double screening.

For the coronation of George III, the duke was appointed, for the second time in the family history, Lord High Constable of England. In this office he had to ride into Westminster Hall, and had new robes made for the occasion. They required twenty-seven yards of rich mantua at six and sixpence a yard, but the thrifty duke used ermine from old robes, to which sixty skins had to be added at a cost of ten guineas. He bought a coronet in its case for thirteen pounds, two shillings from one Andrew Hunter, who also supplied the coronet for the duchess, who wore a dress made by the Queen's dressmaker, with a hooped skirt of silver stuff and a rich silver coat trimmed with *point d'Espagne*. The dress was flounced with silver net and ornamented with gold and silver tassels.

In politics he had formed an alliance with the Marquess of Bute, the new young King's favourite, and at the end of the Seven Years War was sent as ambassador to Paris to negotiate the peace. He complained that his mission there was restricted by conflicting instructions from home, and the fact that parallel negotiations were being carried on in London with the French ambassador, the Duc de Nivernois. It was on this issue that he broke with Bute. The fourth duke was a courageous and outspoken man, and at a later period openly accused the King of bad faith in continuing to take Bute's advice after George III had undertaken not to do so.

The mission to France was by no means a calamity from the personal point of view. The superb set of Sèvres china at Woburn, the most nearly-complete of the only three of its kind in existence, was presented to the fourth duchess before they left by Louis XV himself. The Bedfords also brought back some rather splendid pieces of French furniture, which are still around Woburn.

He very nearly had Bedford House burnt down round his ears in 1765, after he had opposed the bill for imposing high duties on Italian silks. This was intended to shut foreign silks out of England altogether, and the duke was considered to have spoken with uncommon harshness of the Spitalfields weavers, a group of whom hissed him and pelted him with stones, one of which wounded him, as he drove back from the House of Lords. The mob made an attack on Bedford House and were only just kept at bay by a large party of friends and a troop of horse. Two or three of the soldiers were wounded and the rioters were not finally dispersed until the arrival of reinforcements. Both the duke and duchess believed, and stated publicly, that the mob had been set on by Bute.

Family relationships completed a curious full circle when

his daughter Lady Caroline married the Duke of Marlborough, great-grandson of the first duke and duchess. In 1764 his son, Francis, married Lady Elizabeth Keppel, daughter of the Earl of Albemarle and his sister's best friend. They soon had two sons, Francis and John, but in the third year of the marriage their father was thrown from his horse while hunting stag in Houghton Park, Hertfordshire, and picked up with a fractured skull. Five months later his widow gave birth to a posthumous third son, named William, but she died very shortly afterwards of a broken heart. There is a portrait of her at Woburn by Sir Joshua Reynolds.

This double calamity was a severe blow to the duke. In his turn, his eyes were giving him severe trouble; there were constant bills for spectacles and in the last years of his life he underwent an operation for cataract. He died in 1771 at the age of sixty-one.

A contemporary appreciation doubtless hit off his character very well:

> In private life, the Duke of Bedford was affectionate and warm-hearted. Hot-tempered, proud, with an inordinately high opinion of himself, he sometimes spoke without regard for feelings of others, but he was thoroughly honest, high-spirited and courageous, had a good brain and plenty of common sense. His speeches were seldom eloquent and often wrong-headed, but they showed knowledge and apprehension of the subjects under debate. He owed his influence in politics rather to his rank and vast wealth than to any personal qualities. Obstinate and ungovernable as his temper was, he was constantly governed by others—his wife, his friends and his followers, and unfortunately for his reputation chose his friends badly and was surrounded by a group of needy and unscrupulous political adherents.

His heir was his eldest grandson, Francis, a child of six. Once more the estates were in the hands of trustees. His widow, Gertrude, became very much the dominating dowager and her life covered an extraordinary span. When Lady Rachel Russell, the wife of the Rye House plotter, died, Lady Gertrude Leveson-Gower was eight years of age. She lived on into the third year of her great-grandson Lord John Russell, afterwards first Earl Russell and the Victorian Prime Minister.

The elder grandson, Francis, the fifth duke, was very much a man of his times. He did get an education and was sent in succession to Westminster School and Trinity College, Cambridge, but, in spite of a long tour abroad, his mind derived precious little advantage from any of it. His chief exploit on his return in 1786, when he came of age, was to take unto himself a mistress in her fifties. This was the famous Lady Maynard, better known as Nancy Parsons who, before her marriage to Viscount Maynard, had already been the mistress of the Duke of Grafton and the Duke of Dorset. The waspish Horace Walpole called her a common creature. She must have been as attractive as ever when she completely captured the affections of the fledgeling fifth duke. He established her in one wing at Woburn, while the dowager duchess, his grandmother, put up a losing rearguard action from another. In the end it was the duchess who had to go, although she lived on for another nine years, dying at the age of eighty. Nancy did not succeed in engaging her young lover's exclusive affections, but he remained her protector until the end of his own short career.

At the age of twenty-four it was said of him that he had never opened a book in his life. When he took his seat in the House of Lords he told Lord Holland that he hesitated to make a speech from fear of exposing himself by using incorrect and faulty English. True to the Whig traditions of his family, he accepted Fox as his political leader and nerved himself to overcome the defects of his education and take part in the debates. Within two sessions he had become one of the most effective debaters in the House of Lords. He had little wit or imagination, but he was a lively and fluent speaker who held the attention of his audience by the force of his arguments. His one great defect, according to

Lord Holland, was that 'he treated the understandings of his adversaries with contempt and the decision and even the goodwill of the audience which he addressed with utter indifference'.

He was a strenuous opponent of the war with France and when a bill for suspending the Habeas Corpus Act was passed in May 1794, the fifth duke was one of the five peers who signed a protest, and then reintroduced in the House of Lords Fox's peace motion, which had already been defeated in the Commons. The Lords threw it out by a vote of a hundred and thirteen to thirteen. The following year when Pitt appealed for a loan of eighteen million pounds to carry on the war, the duke nevertheless permitted patriotism to override his political opposition to the tune of subscribing a hundred thousand pounds. He became one of the intimates of the Prince of Wales and was one of the two unmarried dukes who supported Prinny at his wedding to Princess Caroline of Brunswick. His brother, Lord John Russell, noted the comment: 'My brother told me that the Prince was so drunk that he could scarcely support him from falling.'

He also drew upon himself the thunderous wrath of Edmund Burke by opposing a proposal to grant him a pension. Burke's retort took the form of the famous 'Letter to a Noble Lord on the Attacks made upon him and his Pension in the House of Lords by the Duke of Bedford and the Earl of Lauderdale'. Comparing his own pension with the grants made to the house of Russell, Burke described these as 'so enormous as not only to outrage economy but even to stagger credibility. The Duke is the Leviathan among the creatures of the Crown. . . . Huge as he is, he is still a creature. His ribs, his fins, his whalebone, his blubber, the very spiracles through which he spouts a torrent of brine against his origin and covers me all over with the spray—everything of him and about him is from the Throne. Is it for him to question the dispensation of the royal favour? Mine was from a mild and benevolent sovereign, his from Henry VIII.'

The fifth duke was also the last great embellisher of Woburn. He called in the famous architect, Henry Holland, who, over the course of a number of years, modified many of the interior arrangements, and constructed a terrace along the whole length of the south wing. He also designed the conservatory and the Chinese dairy which stands on its pond by the side of the northern of the two stable blocks designed by Henry Flitcroft. Francis had been nominated a member of the original Board of Agriculture in 1793, and he established at Woburn a model farm for the breeding of cattle and experiments in crop raising. Annual exhibitions of ploughing and sheep shearing were held which lasted for days, and they became one of the more important agricultural events of the Home Counties.

He also decided to demolish Inigo Jones's former Southampton House in Bloomsbury, which had been the family's town residence for more than a century. The pictures and statues were sold on the spot by Christie in 1800, and the gardens demolished. On the site there rose the present Russell and Tavistock Squares. Saved from the wreck were the Canalettos, which were taken down to Woburn and put in what was then the Venetian drawing-room. In order to show them off to the best advantage the west window was blocked up, obscuring the superb view over the park and the fourth duke's pond. It was not until 1955 that I had them rearranged and opened up the window again.

Two years later the duke was dead, after an operation for strangulated hernia caused by too strenuous a game of indoor tennis on his own court. His will must be a record in brevity. It ran: 'I, Francis, Duke of Bedford, do give all my personal estate to my brother, Lord John Russell.'

He was only thirty-seven when he died, but not without honour. Charles James Fox, in moving the new writ for the Borough of Tavistock, vacated by Lord John Russell on his succession, made a long speech in praise of his friend, which was seconded by Sheridan. Fox sent a copy of his oration to the *Monthly Magazine*, with a covering note saying that he had never before attempted to make a copy of any speech which he had made in public. His own handwritten manuscript is in the muniment room at Woburn.

It was also of the fifth duke that Sydney Smith, the famous wit and divine, made his cutting comment: 'A peculiarity of the Russells is that they never alter their opinions; they are an excellent race but they must be trepanned before they are convinced.' I have often wondered if it was a judgment my father ever read or digested.

The fifth duke was the last member of the Bedford family in the direct line to take an active part in the public life of his times. His brother, the sixth duke, made a brief foray into politics when he took office in 1806 as Lord-Lieutenant of Ireland in the Administration of All the Talents, but he resigned a year later and devoted himself almost exclusively, as did all his successors, to the administration of his estates. He was married twice, had nine sons and three daughters, and his chief claim to fame is that the third son of his first marriage, named after him, was Lord John Russell, one of the main progenitors of the Reform Bill of 1832 and one of Queen Victoria's great Prime Ministers. Lord John certainly made the right contacts when he was young. One of his earliest recollections was of a great party playing cards in the Long Gallery at Woburn, with an enormous figure in a cutaway coat, satin breeches and silk stockings, lying back asleep in one of the chairs and snoring loudly. It was Charles James Fox. The little boy was told to creep up behind the chair and tickle the silk-clad legs until the sleeper woke up and stopped snoring. Another of the relics in the house connected with Lord John is the Riesener inlaid table on which he wrote many of his memoranda. In later life he was raised to the peerage, with his own title of Earl Russell of Kingston Russell, taking his name from the manor in the West Country from which it was long erroneously assumed that our forefathers came. He died in 1878 and is also buried at Chenies. His grandson is Bertrand Russell, the philosopher, although I regret to state that I have never met this distinguished member of my family.

Between the sixth and the eleventh duke, my grandfather, the succession gets a little complicated, and as they all lived the same sort of dull, orthodox, uninteresting lives, it becomes a little difficult to tell their activities apart. The sixth duke was the last builder of the family. In 1830 he had Covent Garden market erected at a cost of forty thousand pounds, and also employed Telford and the Rennies to replan and enlarge the Bedford Level. An enthusiastic naturalist, he developed the pines, willows and shrubs in Woburn Park, and continued for some years the famous sheep-shearing contests, becoming in 1838 a governor of the newly-founded Agricultural Society. The following year he died. His second wife's principal contribution to history was the introduction of tea instead of beer at breakfast, each person with their own little individual teapot, a custom which continued right down to my time.

The sixth duke had remained sufficient of an eighteenth-century survival to adopt a distinctly lofty attitude towards his tenantry. It is of his *ménage* at Woburn during some of the hungry years of the eighteen-twenties and -thirties that the story is told of starving people standing outside his dining-room windows and having the remains of his sumptuous meals shovelled out to them. Something of this attitude remained in the family until my day. My grandfather used to crumble great quantities of buns and cakes, certainly about ten shillings' worth, and strew them on the lawn for the birds. Brought up on my father's parsimony and my mother's pittance it used to seem to me quite incredible. Great-aunt Ela at Chorley Wood used to go one better and put out delicious fresh buns and scones for her feathered friends. Many a time when I was young I used to creep out when she was not looking and deprive the creatures of their treat.

Francis, the seventh duke, eldest son of the sixth, married Anna Maria, daughter of Earl Harrington. When Queen Victoria came to the throne, Anna, still Marchioness of Tavistock, was appointed one of her ladies-in-waiting, and at the coronation in 1838 she walked in the procession at

Westminster Abbey. In 1840, by which time she had become Duchess of Bedford, she was in attendance at the Queen's marriage to Prince Albert in the Chapel of St. James's Palace. In one of the display cabinets at Woburn today there is a spray of orange blossom from the Queen's wedding bouquet and a gold bracelet with a miniature of the Queen set in diamonds, a gift from the bride and bridegroom. Later that year they came to stay at Woburn. The company in attendance included the Duke of Wellington, Lord Melbourne and Lord and Lady Palmerston. Anna remained a close friend of the Queen all her life and is also credited with the epoch-making innovation of introducing the habit of five o'clock tea. I am sorry there is nothing more exciting to tell about these nineteenth-century dukes and duchesses, but that was just about the extent of their lives, although there is a well-founded family legend that Anna Maria was the mistress of Landseer.

The eighth duke, William, son of Francis and Anna Maria, died without issue or recorded activities of note, and the title passed to his cousin, Francis Charles Hastings Russell. His father was Lord George William Russell, the second son of the sixth duke—he came between Francis, the seventh duke and Lord John Russell, the Prime Minister.

Lord George William had been a soldier of note, serving with Wellington at Talavera at the beginning of the Peninsular Campaign and with General Graham at the Battle of Barrosa. In 1812 he became an aide-de-camp to the Great Duke and was on his staff at Vittoria and Toulouse. Later he entered the diplomatic service and was British minister in Portugal and then at Berlin.

His wife, Elizabeth Anne, only child of the Honourable John Theophilus Rawdon, brother of the first Marquess of Hastings, was a great beauty. Byron refers to her in *Beppo* as the only woman he had ever seen 'whose bloom could after dancing dare the dawn'. Just for the record, their third son, Odo William Leopold Russell, was also a diplomatist and is best known for his embassy in Berlin from 1871 onwards, where he became a close personal friend of Bismarck. He was then created Baron Ampthill, which is the other title in our family.

The ninth duke was another of the agricultural Bedfords, always experimenting in the fertilizing properties of manures and the breeding of cattle. It was with him that the family first became really rich. Although he was taunted in the press for his neglect of Covent Garden market and other property in the vicinity, he added over a million pounds to his capital when renewing the leases which fell due in the Bloomsbury estates.

He married Lady Elizabeth Sackville-West, and in the portrait we have of her at Woburn, she is wearing the famous Bedford pearls. We have no idea when or how these came into the family, but they cost an awful lot of money in insurance and, of course, their value goes down every year. In later life the ninth duke became a pronounced hypochondriac and in 1891, in a fit of delirium, while suffering from pneumonia, shot himself at his house in 81 Eaton Square. He was succeeded by his elder son, George William Francis Sackville Russell, who outlived him by only two years, dying without issue. The title passed to his brother, my grandfather, Herbrand Arthur Russell, who, as eleventh duke, started the break-up of the family estates. Not only did he dispose of the Covent Garden properties, but he also sold the Bedford Level and Thorney estates. The task of fighting for what remains has fallen to me.

CHAPTER SIX

STRIFE WITH FATHER

I MUST admit that I had not picked up all this information at the age of nineteen, but I had acquired enough of the background to be able to contrast the large existence of my family with my own solitary and impecunious situation. The period up to the war consisted chiefly of further guerrilla warfare with my family. It sharpened into a complete break, which included being disinherited by my father, on the occasion of my first marriage. For a few months after my grandmother's death, my life continued much the same. I made another half-hearted attempt to get along with another tutor, but I was in danger of becoming the eternal student by now, and I am afraid social life had me firmly in its grip.

The period preceding the coronation of King George VI brought an absolute flurry of parties. I remember one enormous dinner given by Lady Londonderry for the Duke of Sutherland's ball. Everybody who was anybody in London was there—from King Farouk to the Duke of Alba —royalty, politicians and most of the diplomatic corps. I was standing next to one of the ladies at the huge reception, and you had to curtsey and bow to every other person coming in. I got rather confused and very much in need of a drink. The lady next door to me had been curtseying so often that when the next representative of minor royalty came past and she did a duck, I found myself curtseying too. Fortunately no one noticed.

I disgraced myself further at dinner. I was sitting next to quite an attractive girl and in desperate search of something to say I remarked to her: 'Who is that pompous-looking man with a moustache?'—'That's my father,' she said. I

Woburn Abbey today: the West Front from the park serves as our private entrance, as opposed to the half-crown side of the operation, which is entered from the north. Flitcroft was the architect

THE following pictures are hung in what is known as the 'Dukes' Corridor' but what I sometimes call the 'Rogues' Gallery'. Here I have hung the portraits of my ancestors in the direct line of descent, in their chronological order. Here look down on me the men and women who have lived (often outrageously), loved (sometimes unfortunately), bred and died here. They have loved Woburn as I do, and have handed it on to me as I hope to hand it on to future generations. It is a strange sensation, all those centuries of eyes looking at me. They seem to be like my conscience and saying, 'Well, we looked after it for you, now it's your turn to carry on the tradition.' I believe Woburn to be a great incitement and challenge, and should my family lose it much of the incentive to be a worthy Duke of Bedford would be lost. Our roots would be gone, and we would become like so much aristocratic thistledown drifting around the world with others who have lost their family houses and roots. I am grateful for and respect the memory of these ancestors of mine, though some were singularly eccentric, to say the least. . . .

*Francis the firſt by name
Earle of Bedford.*

(*Left*) Sir John Russell, first Earl of Bedford (1486–1555), Lord Privy Seal in the reigns of Henry VIII, Edward VI and Mary. To this one-eyed old man I owe Woburn. This is as Holbein saw him. (*Right*) The second earl (1527–1585) was said to be the ugliest man in England. He got the Order of the Garter like eight others of

(*Left*) Lucy Harrington (1582–1627), wife of the third earl. When her husband was confined to his estates after the Essex rebellion, Lucy continued to live the gay life at Court. Here she is in a fancy dress designed by Inigo Jones. (*Right*) The fourth earl (1588–1641) built the first family house at Woburn on the site of the Cistercian monastery. He was the author of several religious works which he required to be read by his descendants. One at least has not done so

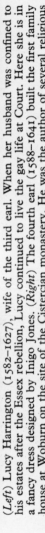

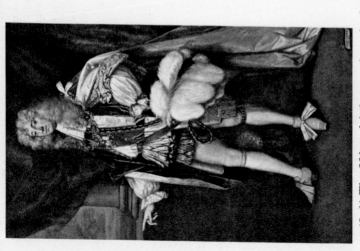

(*Left*) The fifth earl (1613–1700) received a dukedom as a kind of apology for his son's execution. He was the first Duke of Bedford. (*Right*) Anne Carr (1620–1684) whom the fifth earl married, despite family opposition on account of her mother's murderous leanings—a tendency which fortunately has not survived to later generations

(*Left*) This is the fifth earl's murderous mother-in-law, Frances, Countess of Somerset (1599–1632). A revealing portrait. (*Right*) William, Lord Russell (1639–1683) was executed at Lincoln's Inn Field, but not before he had married the daughter of Lord Southampton who brought Bloomsbury as part of her dowry

(*Left*) Rachel (1636–1723), daughter of Lord Southampton, whose husband, William, Lord Russell, was involved in the Rye House Plot. After his execution she set about proving his innocence—to her satisfaction, but not to mine. (*Right*) The second duke (1680–1711) married another heiress who brought him Streatham, Tooting, and a son who gambled most of this cosy dowry away

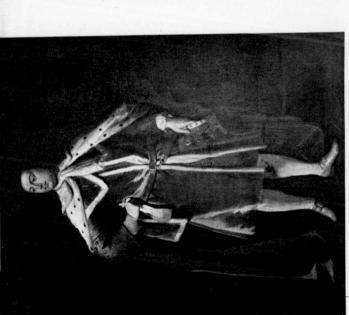

(*Left*) The pompous third duke (1708–1732) gambled away most of his mother's dowry. Fortunately, he died when he was twenty-four before he got through the lot. (*Right*) The fourth duke (1710–1771) did most for Woburn. He rebuilt three sides of the Abbey in 1760, and bought most of the best china and furniture we have today

(*Left*) Gertrude (1715–1794), wife of the fourth duke, was a determined lady with good taste in furniture and about the house generally. She loved gambling and politics. Horace Walpole disrespectfully called her 'the Old Begum'. (*Right*) The fifth duke (1765–1802) was my favourite predecessor. Orphaned as a child, and brought up by his grandmother, he lived in the grand style, acquired a mistress thirty years his senior, maintained a wide

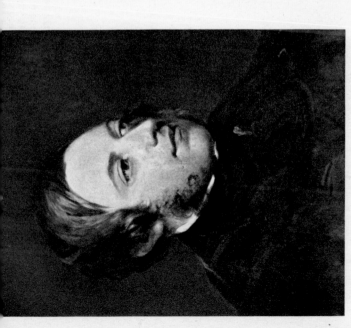

(*Left*) The eighth duke (1809–1872), a bachelor with a promiscuous and inconstant taste for women and a preference for the bright lights of London. Contemporary memoirs describe him as 'sly and sickly'. I wonder. (*Right*) The ninth duke (1819–1891), my great-grandfather. He was a shy, introspective man, convinced that people only liked him for his money. This is possible

(*Left*) My great-grandmother Elizabeth (1818–1897) frightened everyone. She was one of Queen Victoria's bridesmaids and bought a lot of hideous carpets with which we still have to live. (*Right*) The tenth duke (1852–1893) was my great-uncle. One of the shy Bedfords, he had no time for women, but got himself compromised into marriage

(*Left*) My great-aunt, Adeline (1852–1920), wife of the tenth duke. She and her sister, who was coerced into marriage with a homosexual, did good works and doted on children. This was a pity, since they never had any. (*Right*) My grandfather, Herbrand (1858–1940), was the eleventh duke. A selfish, forbidding man, with a highly developed sense of public duty and ducal responsibility, he lived a cold, aloof existence, isolated from the outside world by a mass of servants, sycophants and an eleven-mile wall

(*Left*) My grandmother, Mary (1865-1937), filled her life with fishing, shooting, nursing, flying, bird-watching—indeed, anything to escape from the chilling formality of my grandfather's isolated existence, which she detested, and from her own loneliness, caused by deafness. (*Right*) This is my father, the twelfth duke (1888-1953), the loneliest man I ever knew, incapable of giving or receiving love, utterly self-centred and opinionated. He loved birds, animals, peace, monetary reform, the park and religion. He also had a wife and three children

The State Dining-Room with Van Dyck portraits on the walls and knives and forks stitched to the table-cloth to discourage souvenir hunters

The Library is used as our chief sitting-room in our own quarters. There are a number of self-portraits around the walls including those of Hals, Rembrandt, Cuyp, Reynolds, Murillo, Tintoretto, Hogarth, Steen, etc.

The Canaletto Room with its twenty-three views of Venice. I have opened the Venetian window at the end, blocked by the fifth duke, because I love the view beyond of a lake and an avenue reminiscent of Versailles

The Saloon is the principal drawing-room of the house and
one of the rooms shown to visitors

looked wildly around the table to see if there wasn't another man with a moustache and there wasn't a single one. I had been referring to the Duke of Portland and the girl next to me was his daughter, Lady Margaret Cavendish-Bentinck. It was pretty much of a conversation stopper.

For the actual coronation I had been made a Gold-Stick-in-Waiting and although I received a medal for it, it actually meant that you acted as a peeresses' lavatory attendant. We had rehearsals for weeks and weeks before in which we did absolutely nothing. As there was no one for us to look after yet, the exact nature of our duties remained somewhat unclear.

On the great day we had to turn up in Court dress, velvet breeches and agonizing new pumps at about half past three in the morning. It was five hours or so before any of the guests arrived, and by the time the ceremony started my feet were in such agony that I forgot all about my duties. To make things worse somebody had lost the key to the lavatories, and for about half an hour they all had to use buckets until we broke down the doors. There were plenty of eager young colleagues to look after embarrassed peeresses, and I found myself spending most of the time wandering around the Abbey. I certainly got a much better view of the proceedings than the people jammed in the pews. We Bedfords have no hereditary duties at coronations or royal occasions and since the ninth duke have had practically no contact with the Court at all. I hope the services of our ancestors help to redress the balance.

The other new acquaintance I made in those years was Lord Beaverbrook. I met him through Lady Cunard and went to one or two lunches and dinners at Stornoway House, which I found rather frightening. Part of the company always consisted of bright young men like Randolph Churchill and Michael Foot, and I found myself completely out of my depth. Max Beaverbrook used to explode conversational bombs amongst them and then sit back and enjoy the fight. For some reason he has remained a constant friend over the years, and on one or two trying occasions has been a great help.

The court jester of his circle was Valentine Castlerosse, who had the most fantastic and inexhaustible repertoire of stories about people and things I have ever heard. He could keep a room full of guests in fits of laughter for hours. His wife, Doris, took pity on me once. We were fellow guests at a dinner-party, it was winter-time and I had no overcoat, and no money to buy one either. They gave me a lift home and as we got into the car she said: 'Where's your over-coat?'—'Oh, I left it behind,' I replied.

She was much too sharp to swallow that. 'You haven't got an overcoat, have you?' she said. 'No,' I admitted, 'you're quite right.' She scribbled a note on her card and then said: 'You go to-morrow to this address, buy an over-coat and put it on my account.' It was a very nice gesture. On the one hand she was a *grande mondaine* in the full tradi-tion and at the same time extremely generous and warm-hearted.

One result of my acceptance in these exalted circles was that I had my allowance increased—from ninety-eight to a hundred and forty-four pounds a year. As I recall, even Mrs. Samuel had realized that I could not possibly make ends meet on less than two pounds a week and it was she who added her voice successfully to the volume of remonstrance from friends and relations that thundered round my father's ears. So in a sudden fit of generosity he made it up to twelve pounds a month. It barely paid for the flowers I had to send to my hostesses.

My situation had been further complicated by the fact that I had developed a propensity for falling in love. My first passion was an incredibly beautiful blonde German countess. I had gone into Keith Prowse one day to buy a gramophone record, and in walked this apparition with two young men. I thought she was the most wonderful thing I had ever seen in my life. I had caught sight of her on two or three occasions previously round town without ever speaking to her or finding out who she was. On the spur of the moment I went out and into the flower shop next door, bought some orchids—I was feeling rich on the increase in my allowance—went back into Keith Prowse, told one of the assistants to give them to the girl and cleared out in a panic. The next day I met her at a party and we got on famously.

She lived at the Ritz and as far as I could make out had unlimited money. She surrounded herself with young men, always travelled around in huge Rolls-Royces and Mercedes, and gave enormous parties at which the champagne flowed in buckets. I became a fairly favoured member of her retinue, and went down to a house-party in the south of France with her. It all seemed the acme of the glamorous life to me and I was very flattered to be made a part of it.

This was my introduction to the rich Riviera set who were, heaven knows, a pretty bizarre group of people. It was all like something out of Phillips Oppenheim or Somerset Maugham. There was one very rich American woman who gave the most sumptuous parties while we were there, and involved us all in her private life. She had married a young man who escaped from her embraces from time to time to engage in smuggling cruises from or to North Africa. In the end he was killed in some foray. He had the most ingenious method of getting his wife to finance these expeditions. She was a backgammon fiend, but not very good at the game, so he used to stay at home for a few weeks, win thousands of dollars and then be off on his trips, leaving the good lady in permanent floods of tears. As soon as he found himself short of money again, back he came and down they would sit at the backgammon board. I was pop-eyed at all this and dazzled at the company I was keeping.

Nevertheless the countess was soon superseded as the dominating influence in my life. I found myself falling in love with a woman thirteen years older than myself, whom I found the most sophisticated and delightful person I had ever met. After this loveless childhood and upbringing of mine I do not doubt any number of psychiatrists will consider all sorts of theories confirmed, but she was the first person who really took me outside myself and forced me to become a person in my own right. Her name was Clare Hollway. She was still married when I met her. But although she remained on perfectly friendly personal terms with her husband, they had lived their own lives for years.

We met at a party given by an immensely rich lady named Mrs. Cottingham, whose acquaintance I had first made during my skiing holiday, when she had a chalet at Wengen. Her first husband made Berger's paints and then she married Mr. Lilley, who makes all the shoes. She gave lavish parties where I seldom saw any of the titled people who had launched me into London society, but I found her guests much more vital and interesting than those provided by my more formal social contemporaries, and the possession of a title probably made me more welcome where the competition was less. However, that is a retrospective comment.

'Brownie' Hollway was one of the most vivid members of this coterie. She was extremely elegant, always wore beautiful clothes, had a lovely slim figure and beautiful hands, immense self-assurance and an inexhaustible fund of mother wit. I was completely dazzled by her. Her father had had a certain amount of money, but he had died early, and back in 1925 she had married Kenneth Hollway, who was a Lloyd's underwriter and very comfortably off, but had been quite unable to keep up with this bird of paradise of a wife. She had had a minor career on the stage, and was a contemporary and great friend of Sylvia Hawkes, later Lady Ashley, with whom she went round a good deal.

The good Kenneth was one of those human angels who let her do exactly what she liked. She led her own life, always had a bevy of admirers in attendance, and I was flattered beyond belief when she accepted me into their company. She was a very strong personality with a very strong character, and people either liked her or loathed her. You certainly could not ignore her.

I made relatively slow progress in her favour, but after one house-party in the country we drove back in the same car, and she started inviting me along to her own dinners and dances and gradually we saw more and more of each other. She was the sort of person who drew all eyes when she entered a restaurant and always attracted a great deal of attention. I was delighted to be even an appendage of such a glamorous woman and she, in her turn, started to try to introduce some measure of order into my own existence. She was a complete contrast to the sort of person I had met so far in my life and I submitted willingly to what seemed her immense knowledge of the world. In her forthright way she started to take me in hand. The contrast between her lovely house in Wilton Street and my Bloomsbury digs was too much for her. 'You're mad to stay in it,' she used to say. 'Clear out, show some authority, use some guts, don't get pushed around any more.' I asked rather tentatively where I was supposed to go, and she said that, provided I got out, she would help me to live, and that the most important thing was to show some real independence.

I was so infatuated by now that I think if she had told me to go and live in Timbuctoo I would have gone. So, one day, with a fine show of bravado, I swept out of Mrs. Samuel's establishment and, after a few days in the Cumberland Hotel, was invited to stay with two sisters of Sir Claude Russell, Flora and Diana, who had a house in Oxford Square. I think the peripheral members of my family rather approved of this break, and another cousin, Lady Victoria Russell, said that she would put me up, so I took gross advantage of her kindness and used her house as my home for several months.

Needless to say, this escape from the atmosphere of international brotherhood provoked a pretty sharp reaction from my father. He wrote to me at the beginning of 1938:

If your new friends are so much better than those I found for you and are so sorry for you living under the conditions I arrange that they help you to move your things in order to escape from them, I am rather surprised that they have not gone further and found you a job and that you have not taken it as a means of retaining your liberty. In any case the position is quite simple. If you want any financial help you must comply with my wishes, behave decently to my and your friends and fall in with

117

the arrangements that are made for your benefit. Otherwise you must either continue to live on your friends or earn your own living.

We had a very unpleasant interview shortly afterwards, down at his gabled monstrosity at Haywards Heath, with all the parakeets shrieking out in the aviaries. I so far lost control of myself in the argument that I started to cry, which is not a particularly manly thing to report, but I was so frustrated and furious with him that my emotion got the better of me. Then of course I felt ashamed and when I went out of his room I met Mrs. Samuel, who had doubtless come down for the occasion, and pretended that I had put the act on. Needless to say she reported this to my father, and on my return I received by post another of his long harangues about my general deceitfulness and dishonesty.

Another single-sentence rumble came from my grandfather, who wrote about my 'staying too long and making a nuisance of yourself at Beaufort Gardens'—which was Lady Victoria Russell's home, but there was a temporary truce while I celebrated my twenty-first birthday. Celebrated is a *façon de parler*, as neither my father nor grandfather turned up at all. First of all I had asked if I could have a dance at Woburn, and when this was turned down as being impossible, suggested a party in one of the Belgrave Square houses. This again was ruled out for no apparent reason. I had in the meantime inevitably run up a certain number of debts around London, chiefly to keep pace with the sort of entertainment I had been receiving, so we compromised on a suggestion that these debts should be paid, and that I should hold my twenty-first birthday party in an hotel.

The immediate family complications were too awful. 'Do you think it would be a good arrangement for me to come to the dinner,' my father wrote, 'and for Mummy to come later in the evening for the dance after I had left? It might be the easiest way out of a rather difficult situation.' In the end neither of them came, and my grandfather finally cried off just before the date in one of his tersest epistles: 'I am very sorry I cannot attend your birthday dinner as I am going to Endsleigh next Monday.' About forty Russell cousins came and a few of my personal friends—the first piece of return hospitality I had been able to give them, and either my father or grandfather picked up the bill.

So here I was, duly come of age, next heir but one to one of the oldest titles and largest fortunes in England, and still living on the allowance of an impoverished student. Now that I am older and wiser I would not expect to rate any sympathy in the matter, but it is necessary to cast one's mind back to the conditions twenty years ago. I had never done any work, I had never been brought up to do any work, for several generations the holders and heirs of the title had never done any work, apart from administering the estate sufficiently well to ensure that they did not have to, and, rightly or wrongly, I did not see why they should expect me to behave any differently.

My only recourse, to keep up with the titled Joneses, was to run into debt again and see whether I could borrow any money on the expectations of my inheritance. This caused an ugly exchange of correspondence with my family and brought things to a head. My grandfather wrote in one of his longest letters:

I understand you refuse to write and say you are aware you cannot raise money on your expectations of succeeding to the Bedford estates. You must succeed to the title but you do not succeed to anything else. I tell you this although it has already been explained to you and you know it perfectly well. It is for you to decide if you prefer not to have your debts paid for you and not to receive an adequate allowance for the sake of refusing to recognize what is true and a fact beyond dispute. If you decide to do so you must take the consequences, which means you will be taken into court.

Then an arrangement was made a few months after my twenty-first birthday that I should receive a thousand pounds a year out of my father's share of the estate. This opened up completely new prospects. It also coincided with something of a show-down with Brownie Hollway. By now she had grown as fond of me as I was of her, and although I still continued to see a certain amount of the German countess, Brownie told me pretty sharply that it was time I made up my mind between them. Her husband was perfectly willing to provide the evidence for a divorce, and I remember him coming back from the dreary weekend which supplies the formal evidence in such circumstances, and being very funny about it. I have a warm corner in my memory for him. He continued to pay Brownie alimony even after we were married, and then remarried again himself. Then he had a stroke and died at the age of about forty-five. I can only think he must have a high place in heaven.

Brownie and I became unofficially engaged, and the next problem was to break it to my family. The news caused consternation. I was met by a volley of arguments about marrying someone so much older than myself, marrying someone whose marriage had been dissolved; but their real objection was the fact that they considered I was marrying out of my class. This also seemed to be the opinion of most of the titled people with whom I had been spending a lot of my time, and I was quickly dropped from the guest lists of most of them. I find this sort of snobbery a most unendearing trait, and I cannot say it has encouraged me to seek the company of my fellow peers since.

We went through an awful period while Brownie was 'vetted' at a series of interviews with relations, each more embarrassing than the last. This was part of the delaying tactics instigated by my father. He had one meeting with Brownie. They did not seem to get on too badly and then he wrote:

I leave it entirely to you and Mrs. Hollway to decide whether you care to arrange an interview or not. It did occur to me by reason of something she said yesterday about liking Theo's letters that it might be helpful if you were to see Theo and Marie Louise [these were elderly cousins of mine]. If Theo and Marie Louise did like Mrs. Hollway and felt that the marriage would be wise, their opinion, as you probably know, would have great weight with Miss Greene, who is very fond of them and also indirectly it would help you with grandfather. Neither would it be without value to me. Admittedly at the moment I feel very strongly that the marriage would be a terrible mistake, but my mind is not yet closed on the matter and I have come to no absolutely clear and final decision as yet.

My grandfather proved very difficult and I do not think I can recall my own feelings at the time better than by quoting a letter I wrote to him:

One understands your attitude because in theory the marriage might not prove a success because of the disparity of age. I know if you met Clare you would feel less inclined to hold the view you do because she is such a very wonderful person. She has helped me so much in so many things and made me so happy. Through her example of honesty, loyalty, high ideals and good taste and her endless patience, I have learned what I should like to be and with the help which she gives me, the generosity which is one of her many attributes, I feel confident that I shall accomplish this. It was her beauty and complete naturalness with whomever and wherever she was that first attracted me so much. At the same time she never loses dignity or respect. I am so fond of you and regret what a constant disappointment I must have been to you in the past and that this marriage must be another one.

The meek approach brought no results, so I tried rather more forceful arguments:

There are exceptions to every rule, and where marriage is concerned rules don't seem to apply at all, for marriages that were approved and thought suitable are breaking up every day. I know your marriage was disapproved of the family until they had met grandmother and for some reason nearly every marriage is disapproved of by families. I realize that in my case there may be more than the normal amount of argument against this marriage, but I have gone into every side of the question from every angle and see the arguments against the marriage, and am quite convinced in my own mind that my decision is a right one. I do not like your assuming that Clare might be marrying me for money or that I am the sort of person who might deceive her as to how I am financially placed. She knows my financial position fully and is prepared to 'keep me', though to think why you should wish to place me in such a distasteful and embarrassing position is beyond my comprehension.

This also proved entirely the wrong tack. All I got back was a furious letter demanding to know who had told me that his own marriage had been disapproved of. He pressed this point and ignored all the others, so we reached complete deadlock.

My mother was no better. All she could think of was the possible effect of my marriage on my sister Daphne:

You are of course sufficiently a man of the world to realize that what is perfectly suitable for you and Ma is not seemly for a young girl and that in marrying Clare you make it impossible for Daphne to go about with you. But of course I shall love to see you both when I am alone.

To this I see I replied:

I frankly don't understand the end of your letter in regard to Daphne. Perhaps I have not understood what you really meant. You must realize that I consider Clare as a fit person to meet anyone and particularly so as my wife.

My father continued to write his long homilies, which consisted chiefly of suggestions to discuss our affairs with awful people not really in the family, and to pray for guidance. In the end my future wife refused to submit to any more of the vetting. She had one final disastrous meeting with my father, and being a woman with a fine flow of language who always said exactly what she felt, she called him a miserable old humbug. That was not the way he liked being treated at all, and I do not think they ever met again.

In the middle of all this old Miss Greene died and when she had finally made her mark by being buried in the Russell family vault at Chenies, her place as mistress of all she surveyed at Woburn was taken by a cousin of mine named Marjorie Russell. She seemed a possible new channel of approach, so I fired off another angry letter:

Assuming that I did go against my father's wishes, who told my grandfather I did so and why? Did my grandfather ever hear my side of the question? No. My father is a notorious eccentric and is a complete failure so his wishes are beneath consideration. Even my grandfather is gloomy about the prospect of what is going to happen to Woburn when my father inherits. So he can't think much of him either and would think even less of me, I am quite sure, if I had persistently resigned myself to obeying my father's whims. I expect I should have turned out a strong Oxford Groupist and would be 'changing' the souls of the people of Ohio or somewhere, with a bad smell look on my face and a patronizing manner. But seriously it is not reasonable to ask me to fit in with my father's ideas. Even my mother could not stand them and she is placid enough.

There seemed nothing for it but to go ahead and announce our engagement officially. We were married almost immediately at Caxton Hall, which is a singularly unromantic procedure, rather like buying a dog licence. Of all the family, only Sir Claude Russell and his wife, and two cousins, aunts of the present Lord Ampthill, stood by us. A friend very kindly lent us his suite at the Ritz Hotel before we went abroad on our honeymoon, but he obviously did not want us to pry into his cupboards, every single one of which was locked. We had to hang our things on the mouldings round the doors. The nicest gesture of all came from Kenneth Hollway, who sent in an enormous bunch of flowers with his good wishes.

My father's response was immediate and direct. I received a letter from our banker saying tersely: 'My Lord, We think it well to advise Your Lordship that we have been instructed by the Marquess of Tavistock to discontinue the allowance which we paid to you on his behalf.' I had been cut off quite literally without a penny.

This had been accompanied by a long letter from my father. Our exchanges were pretty offensive, but I think the best way of indicating how complete the estrangement was between us is to give the text of our correspondence in full. On 4 April 1939 my father wrote:

Dear Ian,

I told you that I did not feel it expedient to tell you my reason for discontinuing the allowance if you marry because it might divert my purpose—the promotion of your own welfare. It is sometimes unhelpful to say too many discouraging and critical things to a person and I am afraid that I have already felt obliged to say a good many to you. On fuller consideration, however, and as a result of our talk this afternoon, I feel that perhaps it may be the lesser evil if I am perfectly frank and let you and Mrs. Hollway know the reason for my decision. As I have told you before, I consider that the enjoyment of a substantial unearned income can only be justified if the recipient spends the money wisely and performs some real service to the community which, often at great sacrifice, provides the money. Your grandfather and I, according to our lights and in different ways, have tried to show ourselves not wholly unworthy of our privileges—he by public service, work of value to Natural Science and by certain forms of philanthropy; I, partly in similar ways;

partly by social service and work for the abolition of poverty and war.

You, however, to my great sorrow and disappointment, have, in spite of your opportunities, done absolutely nothing in the way of social service and you have shown yourself, so far, completely destitute of any sense of honour or responsibility in this matter. You have spent your money selfishly and often foolishly; you have not even shown common honesty in paying tradesmen's bills and apart from a few tips to beggars and presents to friends, you have done nothing to shoulder your share of the world's terrible burden or to avert the calamities that threaten all of us more and more darkly. Not only in you but in other members of your mother's family I have observed a quite abnormal degree of selfish laziness; a quite abnormal unwillingness to do anything unpleasant or difficult; and a most unlovely and ungentlemanly snobbishness. These faults, if persisted in, are certain to destroy a man's usefulness and happiness in this life and the next and, when gentler methods have failed, no discipline is too drastic to apply and to *maintain*, for it seems likely that more temporary application would be useless and would only be followed by a relapse directly the pressure was removed.

I have been driven to the firm conclusion that the only thing which, anyhow in part, may save you from yourself and your hereditary handicaps is the necessity of working for your living all your life.

Hitherto, however, I have been placed in some difficulty in this respect, for, good as it would have been for you to have been dependent on your own exertions for your living, it would have been too brutal to leave you absolutely destitute in a world where even well-trained men cannot always obtain work. Your marriage, however, would alter the position and enable me to do what hitherto I have been hindered from doing. I regret to say that I can feel no conviction that Mrs. Hollway is inspired only by sincere affection and is not using you for selfish ends. That being so, I have no scruple whatever, if, contrary to my very earnest appeal she persists in giving me the opportunity, of using her for my *un*selfish ends—the strengthening of your own character. If she marries you, she will provide you with a comfortable home but also from her and from altered circumstances you will receive a continual stimulus to get out of your habitual indolence and apathy. The somewhat unusual but perfectly valid legal arrangements which have been made deprive you of financial expectations in the future—a point which has been established by several lawyers and also by Victor, one of the trustees. For my own part you should know me well enough to realize that I am utterly indifferent to public opinion and gossip so long as I believe what I am doing to be right; accusations of meanness to my son would go like water off a duck's back if I know that my son's unusual temperament left no other wise course open to me. Neither am I moved by the suggestion that it would be unfair to your good name; partly because your past conduct has left you, unhappily, with little further reputation to lose; partly because, unless you choose to talk and complain about it, there is no reason why the world in general *should* know that you are entirely or mainly (if you get a job) dependent on your wife. This is a harsh letter, I fear, old man, but you may one day learn that there are exceptional circumstances when love itself can only express itself truly in the guise of harshness.

Yours affectionately, Daddy.

I took that broadside with me on our honeymoon to the south of France, and when we got back at the beginning of May, I was as frank with him in return:

I cannot see why because I married a girl I happen to love you have to decide that it is the ideal moment to cut me off for the good of my soul. On the other hand, if I had not married my allowance would have continued and my soul go hang as far as you were concerned. . . .

You say that you do not see that an unearned income

should be received by anyone who does not spend it wisely to perform some real service to the community and you mention what you and grandfather have done. You do not mention however that at my age both you and, I think, grandfather enjoyed an enormously greater income than I have ever had which you both received as a matter of course. At my age had grandfather or you completed any social service? Had you commenced to do any social service? I do not think so and you both had large incomes, incomes which went much further in those days than they do to-day. I quite appreciate that both you and grandfather give a lot of time to social service to-day but you are both rich men, you have huge unearned incomes from the money and property handed down by generations of Russells so that you are free from the worry of having to find enough money to live, for food, for clothes and for the hundred and one essentials of life.

If I was in your position and still did nothing your remarks would be justified but until a few months ago I lived on an allowance that is less than you pay your chauffeur. You say that in spite of my opportunities I have done nothing. What opportunities have I had? I do not know of many men of my age, rank and income who can be said to have done social service. If I had an income that was only a fraction of yours, I could devote my time to things such as these, but I do not think your scathing remarks to me on this subject are in any way justified when you realize that I have been treated like a half-witted child by the family and given none of the opportunities that both grandfather and you enjoyed at my age—opportunities to do good. If I had been educated to earn my living or told in my earlier years that I should be expected to do so, one might feel different about your recent action.

It is very difficult at the age of twenty-one suddenly to be told 'You must earn your living for the rest of your life because you have inherited a great many faults and it is the only way you will be saved from damnation'. . . . After all, I did not ask to be born or to inherit faults through my parents. Again I did not ask to receive an education that did not put me on an equal footing with other men. If I had been educated at a school where I should have learnt to mix with other men and not led an isolated existence that did not put me on any equal footing with other men in social, educational or competitive forms then I should feel you might be slightly though only very slightly justified in doing what you have so unfairly done.

Do not think that I have enjoyed my life in the last few years. I have not necessarily enjoyed going to endless dances and dinners but have been driven to them by a feeling of loneliness and desire for company no matter where.

During May we had another acid exchange. My father wrote:

I do not wish to be unfriendly, but at the moment I feel that it might be easier for all of us if I did not meet your wife again just yet. Time in cases like this sometimes opens new roads or relieves tension.

This all seemed so pointless that I was determined to make an end of it:

Frequently in your letters there is evidence of a definite streak of malicious enjoyment that you apparently receive from writing unpleasant things directly or indirectly about Clare, which I naturally will not tolerate. I think it advisable that correspondence between us ceases for the time being. It is most regrettable but you cannot but agree that it is the only reasonable thing to do in the circumstances to prevent there being any definite breach between us.

CHAPTER SEVEN

THE STREAMING COLD GUARDSMAN

I HAD to do something pretty drastic about our situation as soon as we returned from the honeymoon. I could not go on living off my wife's income and hurriedly cast round for a job. I had met one of the directors of Daniel Watney & Sons, the estate agents, while we were in the south of France, and he very kindly said I could join the firm to start learning about land and estate management. It seemed to me the most useful sort of knowledge I could acquire. Neither my father nor my grandfather had ever made the slightest attempt to tell me anything about the administration of the Bedford estates. I suppose that after making up their minds to leave the whole thing in the hands of trustees, they thought the less I knew, the less harm I could do. For all I knew I had been cut off for life, but I could not help feeling that with my grandfather's sense of tradition, some part of the estate would come my way in the end and I had better find out how such things were run.

It was in all conscience a sobering enough apprenticeship. The firm managed a number of estates, and I had to start right at the bottom as a rent collector. I am far too kind-hearted, and would never make a good bailiff's man. A lot of the properties were down in the Stepney area and it was astonishing how many Jewish people could never manage to speak anything but Yiddish when you asked them for the week's rent. I found the whole thing most distressing. I would go round tapping on innumerable doors and half the time the people would say, 'We can't manage it all this time.' Clearly many of them had no money at all, and I felt absolutely awful every time I made them pay up.

I was getting a mere pittance and was probably worth even less. In fact I do not know how we would have survived if the angelic Kenneth Hollway had not bought back from my wife the country cottage they had owned together, and which had come to her under the divorce settlement. Then came the war and he joined up, which meant that the alimony payments he had so generously continued would soon come to an end. I wanted to get into the army myself, but I simply could not go off without making some proper arrangement for Clare. By now we knew that she was going to have a baby. I was already in touch with Colonel Miskin, who commanded the territorial battalion of the Bedfordshire and Hertfordshire Regiment, and we were discussing my being accepted into the regiment. In spite of everything that had happened, I turned to my father again, hoping that the changed circumstances would soften his attitude. He was by now conducting his own public campaign against a declaration of war and would not even consider my request. I am afraid I lost my temper with him. I wrote:

When you were cut off you had fifteen thousand pounds a year, so were not faced with the worries of seeing someone you love already ill and being made worse by money worries. So I suppose it is useless to expect you to understand what it is like having a baby with no money. I cannot imagine why you should feel vindictive towards someone who has given me the only happiness I have ever had and anyway I should not have thought, if you profess to be a Christian, you would allow yourself to have vindictive thoughts about people. However I am sadly learning that the admiration I had for you and the confidence that I placed in your practising what you preached were wrong. Underneath your Christian cloak lies a small, narrow, mean mind, incapable of forgiveness, generosity or feeling. It is a bitter disappointment.

That at least raised a reply, of sorts.

The last thing I want to do at a time like this is to be vindictive towards anyone. But at the moment I feel that other people have more claim than your wife on my money as long as it lasts, which if war does develop may not be very long. Your wife has relatives and friends still able to provide her with the necessaries of life and it is to them I feel she should turn at the present. You yourself, if war does develop, which I still hope God in His mercy may be able to prevent, will have no difficulty in finding paid work of some kind somewhere as long as things are not completely disorganized by destruction. In that hard school you may be able to learn the lessons which you could not learn in times of ease and comfort but which in the long run may make for real happiness.

This was obviously getting me nowhere, so just after the actual outbreak of war I wrote to my grandfather:

I am in a very difficult position and should so like your help and advice as to what you think I should do. Briefly, my difficulty is this—I wish to join the Territorial Army. My father will not approve, being a pacifist, and presumably will not help me financially, which will be difficult enough, but my chief concern is Clare, who is, as you know, having a baby. I am in touch with Colonel Miskin of the Bedfordshire Territorial Army and he has wired me twice to try and arrange to see him, but I have temporarily postponed going to see him as I do not feel I can offer my services until I can rest assured that Clare is properly provided for in my absence or on my being killed. Do you think you could possibly arrange this? I hate to keep writing to ask you for things, but I do not know which way to turn as I know appealing to my pacifist father would be useless.

The idea of my joining the army was something of which my grandfather could approve. I think it was the first thing I had done in my whole life which appeared to cause him pleasure. I also found a useful ally in his estate manager,

Colonel Gordon, who saw to it that my case was put before my grandfather without too much interference from the female cousins who had taken over the running of the household. The duke was by now very old and gradually failing. Like so many of our family, his eyesight had started to go and he was only able to attend to business for brief periods. His first step was to meet the considerable load of debt we had accumulated, and to help us to cut down our expenditure he undertook to pay the outgoings of an inexpensive, draughty and unpractical olde worlde cottage we had found near Reading. Colonel Gordon managed to drop hints to me that some sort of financial provision was being considered, and with this assurance I took the plunge. I started to do basic military training with the Reading University Officers' Training Corps, and fired off letters to anybody I had ever met of any influence to see if they could find suitable military employment for me. I had met Leslie Hore-Belisha, who was the Secretary of State for War at the time, but although he sent a friendly reply to my letter, he made it clear that the only immediate appointments available were for fully trained officers. By now the full terms of the Conscription Act were being applied and as I thought it more creditable to serve as a volunteer I applied to enter the Brigade of Guards as a private. Fortunately my wife knew the Colonel Commandant and the paper work did not present too much difficulty.

I thought it wise to place a couple of facts on record with my grandfather:

> I am afraid that the step I have taken will finally disperse any doubts my father may have had to my being of any worth in his eyes, and I do not like to think of the future. However I feel that what I have done is right and do hope you will too, as I know it is the type of thing of which you approve. Unfortunately Clare is ill and has been in bed for a week. I am rather worried about her, as she has become painfully thin and found it impossible to eat anything without getting terrible indigestion.

I am afraid I had the shortest and most inglorious military

career it is possible to imagine. I was worried to death about money, my wife's illness, her ability to have the baby at all in the condition she was in, and the whole future of our lives. I was probably thoroughly run down when I went to the Guards depôt at Caterham for my medical examination. All the new volunteers had to stand around for four or five hours, stark naked, in this great barn of a drill hall, with all the windows open in the depths of winter. A doctor, who looked to me as if he had a crashing hang-over, stumbled from one to the other of us, sounding chests and tapping knees. Another awful man, with a single hypodermic syringe and a dirty old match-stick with which he rubbed some ointment in, went round jabbing each of us in the arm. The needle got blunter and blunter as he went down the queue and, although he had punctured the first half-dozen neatly enough, by the time he got to the end people's arms were gushing blood.

We stood and stood, absolutely frozen. Now I have never been able to stand the cold. I am too long and thin and bony, and the net result of the day's operations was that I caught the most terrible chill. I was sniffing miserably by the time I got to my bunk, and the next day had a high temperature. That was more or less the beginning and end of my army career, as from that time on it degenerated into a series of sick leaves. It seemed to me a curious method of waging war, to try and kill off your soldiers before you have put them properly into uniform, but that was the way of it.

Training routine for the Guards at Caterham was something which had to be experienced to be believed. I can only assume that the system is devised on the basis that if you oblige a group of men to perform pointless tasks with sufficient frequency they will cease to think for themselves and become well-disciplined soldiers. My chief memory is of swabbing acres of floors all morning to take the polish off, and then spending the whole afternoon putting the polish back on again. Endless square-bashing meant that we were warmer outside in the winter than inside, where the windows were always kept open a regulation eighteen inches. The only merit to be obtained was from folding one's blankets at dawn in a precisely regulated way so that they all acquired exactly the same shape. Our heads were shaved, the food was disgusting beyond all belief, and I can only recall the period now as a continuous frozen nightmare.

Almost the only army records I seem to possess are sick passes, most of them made out in the name of Mr. I. R. Howland or Guardsman I. R. Howland, which goes to show the poor opinion they had of me. I started to wonder whether I had been a little too quixotic in offering my services. Our domestic affairs were still unresolved and Clare was even more unwell than I was. In despair I wrote to my grandfather again asking if she could come up and stay at one of his Belgrave Square houses as the doctor said she must be in London for special attention. In a side note to Colonel Gordon just before Christmas I added:

My father and I are such poles apart and we never agree about anything anyway. If only my grandfather would see this and could decide whether he thinks my father is the right person to decide whether my wife and I are to be left destitute when my father becomes duke. I am sure this will happen if things are left as they stand.

I even wrote to my father again, telling him how worried we were, but he was by now far off in the clouds with his anti-war propaganda and could only answer like this:

The best that can be said for unpleasant experiences is that there is always something to be learnt from them. If, unlike the members of the present government, you are not one of the many fools who are incapable of learning from experience, you may therefore be able to learn something of value from your experiences in the army. We are going to Woburn for a week or ten days. Apart from being glad to do what one can for grandfather, I cannot say I look forward to the prospect of seeing the chances of having to say good-bye to Woburn sooner or later, which are extremely great unless the government and their war can be suppressed at a fairly early date.

This was hopeless, but succour came at the last moment from my grandfather. Colonel Gordon wrote to say that the duke would accept all the expenses of my wife having the baby. Clare was by now pretty desperate about the whole situation herself, and grasped at this straw by declaring that she would have the child in the Ritz Hotel and nowhere else. So we took a couple of suites in the Ritz for several weeks, and when the baby was born in January no one can say that it was not in circumstances in keeping with the status of his family.

In the midst of all this I started feeling worse and worse, and went to a series of private doctors to find out what was wrong with me and get the necessary medical certificates. I see that 9 January, Dr. G. E. Beaumont, a physician at the Middlesex Hospital, noted that although I was six feet one and three-quarter inches tall, I weighed exactly ten stone, thirteen and a half pounds clothed. His comment was almost superfluous: 'His physique is very poor and he must be lacking in reserve power.' Over the next four weeks my family doctor certified that I had suffered from bronchitis, emphysema, complicated by an attack of sinusitis. In March he listed the following symptoms; 'Temperature 104°, pulse 120, respiration twenty-four, enlarged glands in the neck, condition very suggestive of German measles.' Three days later I collapsed, eliciting on my certificate the comment: 'In my opinion Lord Howland is medically unfit for general service in the army.'

We were both at our wits' end when a stupendous piece of news arrived from Colonel Gordon. Although my poor grandfather had had a mild stroke, he had recovered sufficiently to attend to family business. He had signed a deed of covenant undertaking to pay me through trustees the sum of two thousand pounds a year less tax. This arrangement was to be perpetuated in a codicil to his will, which gave me a life interest in the income of forty thousand pounds. Here indeed was what would be riches to most people. It was riches to us in the situation we were in, and I hope what follows will not appear ungrateful.

As far as I knew this was the only share of the vast Bedford estate I would ever get. Relations with my father were so strained, and his behaviour had become so peculiar, that I had no reason to suppose that any further provision would ever be made for myself and my family. Although we could certainly survive under the new arrangement, there was my son to think of. One day he would also inherit the title, and I could not see how I was going to bring him up in a manner befitting his status. It was all a question of categories. Two thousand pounds a year would be a very handsome income for someone with a few obligations, but whether my father and grandfather were prepared to allow me to shoulder them or not, I could not help feeling that one day the maintenance of the family traditions would be in my hands or in the hands of my son. I decided to fight for some greater provision, if not for me, then at least for the boy, and if the squabble appears unedifying then I can only plead that having undertaken to set down the story of my life, there is no point in leaving out pertinent details.

Colonel Gordon had proved the best channel of approach to my grandfather, so in April I wrote him:

It is rather incongruous that an allowance of two thousand pounds a year should be thought enough for us to live on and yet when my father was married he automatically received fifteen thousand pounds a year and has on many occasions had to turn to my grandfather for help as he could not manage to live on that amount. Whatever else my father may be he is not extravagant. He cannot be accused of living in a decadent or lavish style and yet with his fifteen thousand pounds a year he still cannot live within his income. It is strange therefore to me that I, his eldest son and heir, should be expected to live on well under one-seventh of his income. I only ask for what I am sure is a very small share of the great wealth of my family and one which I do not think anyone would call anything but reasonable.

I coupled this with a letter to Marjorie Russell:

Of course grandfather is quite right about the allowance being my father's responsibility, and I am sure we all agree with him on that. My father of course will not see this, as he cannot live within his own income and will not want to increase his overdraft. Of course he won't admit this and will in some way justify himself for shirking his responsibility. As he thinks he holds the divine right it is difficult to alter his opinions. My grandfather of course kicked him out for shirking his responsibilities at the beginning of the last war, but I see that it is difficult to tell grandfather this, although it might be done tactfully.

If my grandfather or father had made the money, one would feel there would be a justification for their behaviour. But I do not see why my son should have to go to a board-school or I should have to live like a clerk when my family's money is squandered on a million and one extravagancies. However, there is no reason why I should impress on you the eccentricities of this strange family of ours, as I am sure you appreciate them fully.

I wonder what my grandfather expects us to do. We all agree that he has done a lot for us and are most grateful, but if he had not got together with my father when I was sixteen and altered the whole entail arrangements of the estate, we should not be quibbling now. This document is the only one of its sort that has ever been drawn up and cost thousands and was concocted for no reason. It deprives the unfortunate Ampthill child of all that should rightly be his among other things, and I have reasons to suspect its origin.

It was all no use. She replied:

I am sorry to tell you that I have come to the conclusion that there is nothing more that I can do for you. Your grandfather has told us more than once that he has done more than his share already. That is his considered opinion and Margaret Ampthill and I feel we have put the case for an increased allowance with all the emphasis we can and that there we must leave it. Your grandfather is not in a fit state now for discussions. He cannot concentrate for long and when it is over he is so perturbed and exhausted that I refuse to do it again.

If that was the case, I felt that I should at least try and see him again, and if possible introduce him to my wife, but when I put this up to Marjorie Russell she replied that she was sure that there was no chance of him receiving us both at Woburn because of his rooted disapproval of divorce. However, in the end he sent a message that he would be pleased to see me provided I came alone and did not discuss my affairs with him.

I found him in a very pathetic condition. He went more or less to pieces after my grandmother died. She must have meant a great deal more to him than he had realized. In spite of the stiffness and formality of their relationship, she had been his last human contact. After she had gone he had ceased to care about anything else. Towards the end he was almost completely blind and had to have a nurse or servant to guide him round the house. When people remarked what a lovely day it was, he would agree almost eagerly although he could not see a thing. At night the rooms were lit up with tremendously powerful bulbs like a film studio so that he could just distinguish his way by the differences of light and shade. He was more than a little senile and longing to die. I made no attempt to discuss my problems with him—it would have been pointless—and only remember one haunting, half-mumbled remark when he complained that euthanasia was not legal.

I had hardly been to Woburn at all since my grandmother's death, so I was interested to see the memorial window they had put up to her. It shows, appropriately enough, the figure of St. Francis, surrounded by every manner of bird. I believe my grandfather drove the people who were making it almost to distraction. No artist's licence whatever had been allowed. All the birds had to have all the right pin feathers and be perfect in every anatomical detail. He used to tell them that my grandmother would not have liked it unless everything was absolutely correct.

He was still living at Woburn all alone, with fifty indoor, and more than two hundred outdoor, servants. Ten rooms were taken up by the six nurses who watched over him in three shifts. The stable blocks had been taken over by one of the secret government departments and there were hundreds of hush-hush people jammed into them. They asked at one point whether they could possibly take over one of the wings of the Abbey as overflow because they were so terribly crowded, and had received a terse reply from my grandfather saying that they did not seem to appreciate that there was someone living in the house, although most of the hundred rooms must have been empty.

My own chronic ill-health still continued. The German measles had been complicated by broncho-pneumonia and the army made up its mind that I was unfit for general training. After light training I was to become an army clerk with the permanent rank of private. Dr. Chance had sent me along for a final opinion to see Lord Horder, who gave his considered opinion in a letter I still possess:

Dear Chance,
    I agree with you that this weedy youth is no good for soldiering. He will clutter up a hospital bed every time. As you know he has done so ever since Christmas. His sinus inflammation has not subsided, he still has some bronchial catarrh, he is a plus plus myope and his blood pressures are 100/60. He can surely get a useful job outside H.M. forces.

A copy of this was forwarded by Chance to the regimental adjutant of the Coldstream Guards, with the unflattering comment; 'His unfitness is due to a congenitally poor physique and an extremely low standard of resistance to infections and to a general lack of stamina.'

I still wanted to do something useful if I could and thought that I might get seconded for some more interesting work in one of the ministries. Lord Beaverbrook had just been made Minister for Aircraft Production, so I wrote to him asking if he could find a corner where I might be useful. His reply was friendly, but he could not help:

> I am sorry that you are not fit enough to be anything but an army clerk, certainly that would be an unsatisfactory way to make use of you in this war. I doubt greatly if you would be a good clerk. I am sure you could be really valuable to the country in some other capacity.

I was to turn to him again with more success very shortly.

I also had a friend at the Dominions Office, to whom I wrote and asked whether there was any likelihood of my obtaining a post on the staff of some Governor-General, but this came to nothing either.

In something of a gesture of defiance, we had the baby christened in the Henry VIII Chapel of Westminster Abbey on 27 May, a ceremony attended only by a few elderly cousins. Then, at the end of July, came this curt note from the Coldstream Guards office: 'We regret to inform you that you were found to be physically unfit for any form of military service and in consequence you will be discharged from the regiment with effect from 31st July.'

Three weeks later my grandfather died. I felt a distinct pang of conscience that in the five or six years I had been allowed to know him I had failed so dismally to build up any human relationship with him. Deep down underneath his formal manner, I think he realized that with his death and the war the life he had known would go for ever. He was bitterly disappointed in his son and his grandson and, looking back at my mass of resentments at the time,

I must take my share of the blame. If there had been a normal family atmosphere from the time of my birth, things might have turned out differently, although whether the temperaments of both my father and grandfather would have permitted any change in the pattern of their and my lives I rather doubt.

There was a great family gathering at Woburn for the funeral, an occasion which provided Clare with her first and only opportunity of seeing the Abbey. Although she might reasonably have hoped that the occasion might result in some form of reconciliation, nothing was further from my father's mind. Various other Russells were civil and polite to my wife, whom most of them were meeting for the first time, but that was all. My father seemed completely incapable of taking control of the situation. He had always been terrified of people, and the sudden responsibility of giving orders to the different heads of departments on the estate, all clamouring for instructions as to how they should act, was quite beyond him. His inability to take any initiative at all saved him from one embarrassment. The King had sent a representative to attend the memorial service at Woburn, but as this was at a time when my father was making rather an ass of himself with his pacifist campaign, the member of the royal household had been instructed not to stay to lunch if he were invited. My father was at such sixes and sevens that he completely overlooked this courtesy, so the intended snub was never administered.

Shortly after we returned to London, I received a letter of condolence from one of the estate managers at Woburn in an envelope with an embossed stamp of Edward VII. They must have bought an immense stock at the beginning of the century, and probably thought it was time they were used up. Owing to war-time conditions, the assessed value of the estate dropped drastically from what it had been worth a year or two earlier. But even leaving out of account what had been settled on my father and other relations, he still left £4,651,371, on which duties of

£3,100,000 were assessed, which were still being paid off when I inherited the title in my turn. As it was my father was now the duke, I had become the Marquess of Tavistock and, for all the good it did me, I might just as well have been plain Mr. Russell.

CHAPTER EIGHT

IN THE NEWS

DURING the years immediately before and after the outbreak of war, my father's eccentric opinions succeeded in making him into a notorious public figure. He had long deluged any newspaper prepared to print his letters with long diatribes about relatively harmless hobby-horses such as monetary reform and the like. As the political scene in the late thirties moved towards its final crisis, his notions became much more controversial. He has, I fear, been tainted by the accusation of having been pro-Nazi. I think if he had ever come out of his dream world to appreciate what the real facts of the Hitler régime were, he would have been horrified. The trouble was that he adopted such a lofty moral tone about his fellow human beings that he seemed to think that Hitler was by no means the worst of a thoroughly bad bunch of political leaders in every country.

As far back as 1936 he had a letter printed in the *Manchester Guardian* in which he wrote that among the chief causes of war danger were 'the absence of any effective machinery for keeping the people of the different countries adequately in touch with one another, stupid, corrupt or ambitious statesmen, dictators and owners of newspapers, who cultivate the idea of a non-existent robber-raider nation which would make an unprovoked attack on an unarmed neighbour, re-armament and the unwillingness of governments and dictators to make any unselfish concessions in the interests of other nations and world peace'—which was also a fair indication of his literary style.

He was more willing than most to give Hitler the benefit of the doubt. As late as 1938 he was almost justifying in other letters Hitler's Sudeten grab, warning of the dangers of an alliance with France and of the inadequacy of the great majority of political leaders to weigh accurately grave moral and practical issues. In October of that year he was still trying to maintain that a certain Hitler speech had proved that reasoned friendliness with him 'begets a like spirit'. The maximum note of disapproval he could bring to bear after the Czechoslovakia *coup* was that it was 'a grave disappointment to those who had hoped that he might confine his territorial ambitions to the people of German race'.

It was during the summer of 1939 that my father took the step, finally disastrous for his reputation, of becoming chairman and founder member of a new political party to be called the British People's Party. His associates were Benjamin Greene, a former member of the Labour Party, and John Beckett, who had also started as a Socialist and then been a member for a couple of years of Sir Oswald Mosley's British Union of Fascists. They even put up a Mr. Harry St. John Philby to contest a by-election at Hythe, although he lost his deposit.

My father had no political judgment whatsoever. Defending Beckett's former membership of the Mosley movement, he could write:

At that time it was a very understandable step to take and many fine English people were temporarily attracted by Sir Oswald Mosley's party, after being disgusted by the corruption and inefficiency of the older parties. Quite apart from the fact that even the European Fascist countries had some excellent features in their social service and economic plans, British Union policy, a statement of which not one in a hundred British Union critics has ever read, also possessed some very attractive features—attractive because they gave promise of more administrative efficiency and more genuine democracy than are possible under the existing system. There are interesting and workmanlike suggestions for the removal of those delays which make parliamentary procedure

144

so slow and cumbrous; considerable support is given to the idea of monetary reform; while the occupational franchise, which divides the electorate according to their trade, profession or occupation, encourages each section to choose representatives who, in addition to promoting national interests, would also possess the expert knowledge needed to protect adequately the interests of their section. Such a plan, if not altogether free from risks and difficulties, would at least tend to raise the standards of efficiency in Members of Parliament and undermine the evils of the party system.

His attitude and his public pronouncements earned him some severe criticism in the press. He got into further hot water just before war broke out by writing letters making disparaging remarks about the Poles. A month after the outbreak of war he joined a new organization styling itself the British Council for Christian Settlement in Europe, which had John Beckett as its secretary, and included in its members Captain Gordon Canning, a former member of The Link, which had been disbanded as an agency of enemy propaganda. There was a first-class row in Parliament, during which Sir John Anderson, who was Home Secretary at the time, made it clear that the new organization was being closely watched and indeed many of the people connected with it were to spend most of the war as 18B detainees in Brixton prison. I can only suppose that my father was spared the same fate either out of reluctance to lock up someone with such an old and respected title or because those in authority recognized his basic futility.

One of his most astonishing exploits was to conduct a private peace offensive with the German Legation in Dublin. He got in touch with them through a Mr. John Gregg, who lived in Belfast and had married a German woman. Gregg and my father were led to believe that the German Government was prepared to allow Czechoslovakia full independence provided she remained neutral, and to make a similar concession in regard to Poland, on the same condition, provided an outlet to the sea with the necessary railway communications and the use of the Vistula was also granted to Germany. They were led to believe that Germany was prepared to disarm provided that all powers interested in an international disarmament pact were willing to do the same. The Germans expressed themselves as ready to join a re-formed League of Nations; they wanted the return of their former colonies; they were prepared to hold a plebiscite in Austria, and undertook to co-operate with an international body to find a national home for the Jews.

This information my father passed on to Lord Halifax, who described his action as 'rather irregular', but in the end gave him permission to visit Dublin to see if the terms were authentic. This he did, about February 1940, only to find that the Germans were becoming evasive. They had been snubbed in their peace overtures just after the outbreak of war and were not prepared to give official sanction to these new approaches. John McGovern, M.P., who had been associated with my father in this enterprise, thought that further delays could best be averted by telling the whole story to the press and this, of course, caused another political storm to break round my father's head. As he had acted with the knowledge of a member of the government, there was very little they could do about it.

I had no contact with him at all during this period and could only shrug in bewilderment when people used to ask me what was going on. I hardly saw him during the whole of the war. Clare and I went through a very difficult period just after my father came into the title, as it took months to sort out even the preliminary details of my grandfather's will, and for a long time we had no money coming in at all. My father shut down the Belgrave Square houses, sacked all the London staff, but then found that the hush-hush people who had taken over part of Woburn refused to have him anywhere near the place in view of the reputation as a security risk that he had gained for himself.

He refused all offers from me to help look after the

storing of the valuable furniture and pictures, and ignored my suggestion that I had learnt enough about estate management to look after the family's affairs. He brought down Mrs. Samuel to take care of the wing of the house where the furniture had been stored and, after living for a time in the village, retired to the shooting estate my grandfather had always rented in Scotland.

As if he had not caused himself enough trouble, he then started to institute divorce proceedings against my mother, but when the rest of the family, including myself, rose up in arms, he did not go through with it.

He was making himself so obnoxious in the public eye that I felt I had to do something about it. After all, he was my father and I did not want to see him in prison. I wrote to him:

> I understand that your various pro-German peace and other political activities, together with the divorce proceedings and various letters you have written opposing the government and army at Woburn have been very greatly responsible for the steps that have been taken. You have antagonized the Court, political circles and the press and though I know you have a poor opinion of all three, they are the most powerful governing bodies in the country and you will find them tough adversaries. Many people are saying that much of what you do is due to your secretary's influence, who is regarded as not the class of person to govern a duke. The rather high position of authority in which you have placed Mrs. Samuel at Woburn has done your reputation a lot of harm too.

I could have saved my paper and ink. At the beginning of 1941 he was off on another tack. One of our oldest family obligations had been to pay the vicar's stipend at Woburn Parish Church. My father had made up his mind that the Church of England was supporting the war and decided to stop these payments and join the Plymouth Brethren. He wrote to me:

147

I feel unable to continue to support the Woburn Church in the way grandfather did, partly because war taxation has enormously reduced my income, partly because I intend to leave the Church of England and partly because the Church of England as a body supports the war. War has been aptly defined as 'mass murder and organized sin' and a church which even after the lesson of the utter uselessness of the last war continues to support mass murder and organized sin, is so disloyal to its founder that it is unworthy of support at a time when more deserving organizations and individuals badly need it.

The public announcement caused another uproar. The Bishop of St. Albans challenged his right to cut off the stipend, and the ecclesiastical authorities started delving back into documents dating from the Middle Ages to prove that my father could not get out of the obligation. In the ensuing press controversy, someone wrote a letter saying: 'What on earth would the Duke say if one of his tenants declined to go on paying him rent because he objected to his political activities?'

Things got so bad that I felt I had to make some gesture to retrieve the family honour, so my wife and I went down to pay a courtesy visit on Archdeacon Martindale the day before he left the vicarage. He had been found another living. Years later when I had come into the title myself, I saw to it that our trustees reassumed the family obligation.

The family was being called so many names that I had to spring to their defence myself. I wrote a letter to the *Star* pointing out that the Plantagenet Duke of Bedford of 1422-51, whom they described as the brigand who had founded our fortunes, was in fact no relation, and even found myself defending my grandfather and great-grandfather by drawing attention to the millions of pounds they had spent on improving houses and schools on our estates.

Although my father's name was linked with the arrival

of Hess in Britain, I cannot see how he can be connected with the affair. Hess may have thought from his reputation that he might be a suitable person to contact, but apart from the Dublin visit, my father had had no relations with any Germans of importance and had not visited the country. That did not prevent Mr. Herbert Morrison later in the year getting up in Parliament and saying: 'There is a noble lord, a member of the other house—I have not put him under detention and I am not saying anything about him—except that I am interested in him and his activities —who, as long as I am Home Secretary and as long as his opinions and activities are what they are, will not go to Dublin. That is the Duke of Bedford.'

My father got crankier and crankier as the war went on, surrounding himself with more and more peculiar people and making the rest of the family squirm with embarrassment for him. He deluged all sorts of people with a series of pamphlets, with such titles as *Don't be a Gull; Why Blunder On; The Financiers' Little Game; Why Not Think; What a Game*, although where he got all the paper from in war-time is a mystery to me. He was also running a periodical called *The Word*, in which, as late as the end of 1941, he was still writing of Hitler as 'an untested man whom it is neither necessary, sensible nor right to quarrel with until he has been tested by the one test which to me is worth anything, that of wise, practical and genuine friendliness.'

The landlord of his shooting estate in Kirkcudbrightshire, Mr. James McKie, M.P. for Galloway, terminated his tenancy, and he was subject to other public humiliations. He was refusing to have the railings round Russell Square, Bloomsbury Square and Bedford Square removed under the Defence Regulations and one night the statue of our ancestor in Russell Square was defaced. Part of the face was painted yellow, a red, white, and blue ribbon was hung round the neck, an empty paint tin planted upside-down on the head and a bottle with a paint-brush attached to its right hand. Such signs as *Grandfather of a Quisling,*

Down with the Duke and the Railings and the yellow V-sign were daubed all over it. His views were described by Lord Simon, then Lord Chancellor, in the House of Lords as 'utterly irresponsible and completely pestilential'. As if in reply, he sent a football for the use of the 18B political detainees in Brixton.

About the middle of 1942 I received a letter from him which just about summed up our situation: 'As far as I can judge,' he wrote, 'we now live in quite distinct worlds and there is hardly any point of real contact between the two'. There seemed indeed nothing I could do to save him from himself.

He remained absolutely convinced that he was unquestionably right in everything he said and did. He appeared from time to time to address the House of Lords, although most of his fellow peers used to get up and walk out the moment he rose. In his pedantic, high-pitched voice, he would say his piece, sit down and then leave the Chamber immediately. Later in 1942, when he made an attack on the Prime Minister and American arms firms, the oldest peer present, Lord Gainford, took the extreme course of moving that as the duke had declined to be relevant to the debate he should be 'no longer heard'—a procedure which I believe had not been used since time immemorial. Even two years later, Lord Bruntisfield, replying for the government to a speech he had made on war aims, described it as 'verging on the subversive'.

He was also in continuous trouble with the War Agricultural Committee about the valuable herds of rare animals in Woburn Park. He was accused of diverting huge quantities of fodder for their upkeep, and of refusing to plough up enough of the land for productive purposes. In the end he sacked the farm manager, Mr. Henry Hobbs, who had been with my grandfather for nearly fifteen years, and had been prepared to accept a reduction in the deer and bison herds. This led to a lawsuit between them, and another public scandal. However, in the end, an uneasy compromise was reached. At least my father's obstinacy resulted in retaining more than sufficient breeding animals to maintain the herds which still grace the park to-day.

For the last three years of the war I had practically no contact with him at all. I had enough problems of my own. We had struggled somehow through the period after my grandfather's death, chiefly by living on credit at the little cottage near Reading my grandfather had subsidized for us. I was still feeling pretty shaky after several months of severe illness, and my wife never really recovered from the poor health she had contracted while having our first-born. We spent the miserable months of the winter of 1940 shivering behind the porous walls of this ramshackle house, while I cast around for something to do. The forces would not look at me, I did not appear to have the qualifications for any government appointment, so in desperation I turned again to Lord Beaverbrook.

His response was immediate. He gave me a job on the *Sunday Express* as a reporter and told me to get in touch with John Gordon, the editor. They must have been pretty short of trained journalists or I would never have got inside the door, and I do not think that Gordon was particularly pleased to have anyone quite so useless planted on him. I was not made excessively welcome and after our first meeting I saw very little of him. I had to do my share of the run-of-the-mill work with the other reporters and I do not suppose I was ever paid more than about ten pounds a week, but at the time it seemed like a fortune.

People say many hard things about Max Beaverbrook, although he gives as good as he gets and needs no defence from me. He is often accused of having a poor opinion of his fellow peers, but I can only say that on the two or three occasions when I have turned to him for help and advice he has never failed me. He gave me a job when I had no money and no qualifications to write or do anything else, and I shall always be very grateful. He had nothing to gain by it, and no attempt was made to exploit my name in the by-lines of the paper.

I enjoyed the work very much. I adore news and change.

Every day was different and, as I have rather a gossipy nature, I was in my element. It was one of the best things that has ever happened to me. I had always been rather shy and you cannot be a reporter and be too shy. Also it taught me, however much you may not like a person, if you want to get a story out of him, you have to be nice to him. I got on extremely well with my colleagues and was delighted to find them the sort of people who accept you at your face value. There is absolutely no snobbery and a wonderful camaraderie in the press world. There is a pleasantly raffish and spontaneous atmosphere in the profession and I still look back with nostalgia to the convivial drinking sessions we used to have at El Vino's, the Press Club and in the pubs off Shoe Lane. It is perhaps because I have such pleasant memories of these war-time years that the press finds me so easy to deal with to-day. I know their problems from personal experience and know that if you play fair with a newspaper reporter he will never let you down.

I used to find my title gave me a very useful *entrée* when I was sent out on stories, but in the beginning I was given all the routine stuff to do. I used to get sent to an awful lot of ghastly public lunches and dinners, where I was supposed to listen to all the speeches and make a note of the important points. When you are full of cocktails and food, you are already half-asleep, and I used to find only too often that when the important point came it went straight over my head. Then the agencies would pick it up, and there was hell to pay if I had missed it. My saviour was the news editor's secretary, whose name was Miss Murray. It took me ages to learn to type and she used to take my handwritten copy, put it into proper form and dash it off in her typewriter at lightning speed.

Having been brought up to mind my own business and not stick my nose in other people's affairs, I was horrified at the first outside assignment they gave me. I was sent down to Hampton Court to ask a lady how she had come by a grace-and-favour apartment. I knew her husband had only recently been killed in the war, and I practically sweated blood going down, wondering how on earth I was going to ask her such impertinent questions. However, I rang the bell and I must say she was most helpful and co-operative. I think she must have realized how embarrassed I was. It was Lady Kennedy, Ludovic Kennedy's mother, and her husband had won the V.C. in the *Rawalpindi*. Years later I was able to repay her kindness when Ludovic came to interview me for an article he was writing.

One of the most amusing examples I had of sheer force of personality was when I had to go and interview Lady Louis Mountbatten. It looked at one time as if there was some tremendous scandal brewing in the St. John Ambulance Brigade. Two or three of the titled ladies at the top were furious with each other about something, and I was sent to ask Lady Louis what all the trouble was about. It was one of the best lessons I ever had of someone in that sort of position making use of newspaper people. She did not answer one single question I asked, and talked instead at persuasive length about any number of other things, including a long story about a department of the brigade which needed additional funds. She made it all sound so interesting that in the end I went away quite happy to write the story she wanted, for which I certainly took my hat off to her.

I gradually learned to forget practically everything I had been taught about writing English, and started getting my information into short, sharp sentences. The only real *coup* I ever remember bringing off was when General Carton de Wiart had returned from a trip to Yugoslavia or somewhere he had been to negotiate an exchange of prisoners. He was the first person to have been behind the enemy lines and every reporter in London was out to find out where he was to get the story. All the big names were searching London for him, and simply by ringing up his club and asking the porter, which seemed to me the basic thing to do, I found out where he was and got the story. This sent my stock up quite a bit. Several other papers rang up and more or less offered to bribe me to pass on the information, but I refused.

From then on relations with John Gordon became a little easier, but even so, when I was asked to do stories about people whom I knew, I always saved myself from final embarrassment by pretending that I had made a mess of it and had failed to get the information.

I was doing this five days a week, getting up at Reading at the crack of dawn, travelling up in the train, and often not getting back until well after dark. In addition, we had all the usual fire-watching duties round the *Express* building, and although the irregular hours and all the travelling involved quite a strain, I enjoyed every minute of it.

One or two of the friends from my debs' delight days were still around in London, but most of them had gone to ground for the war. Lady Cunard had come back from her native America, where she had spent two or three years, but as she used to go out of her way, between the wars, to say rather nasty things about her rich fellow Americans, they had not been very nice to her when she rejoined them. She had never invited them to her house in the old days and now she had got something of a cold shoulder in return. She moved into a suite in the Dorchester, which she furnished with her own belongings, and tried to get her *salon* going again. She used to give large lunch- and tea-parties, but even she no longer had quite the same amount of money to spend and the atmosphere was never the same.

As our finances came under control again, and the bombing eased, Clare and I got our furniture out of store and opened up the house at Wilton Street again, but with the coming of the doodle-bugs we moved back to the country for the sake of the children. By then we had a second son, born in March 1944, whom we christened Rudolf. It was shortly after this that Clare's health started to give way. Things got so bad that I had to give up my job with the *Sunday Express* and concentrate on acting as nursemaid and housemaid. There were no servants to be had and in any case we could not afford them. I used to go out and do all the marketing, buy all the food, cook the meals, and generally act as nursemaid. I gave up trying to do it at Wilton

Street, with its five flights of stairs, and we had to stick it out at the nasty little cottage in the country, which was easier to run, in the hope that she would get better. Even so it was one dreary round of getting up at the crack of dawn to stoke the boilers, doing all the chores and washing those endless nappies. I do not think I shall ever be able to look at babies' clothes again.

Clare was thoroughly run down, but the real trouble began when she started getting a series of boils and abscesses in her ears. This was before the days of penicillin. She was in awful pain and the wretched boils kept reinfecting themselves the whole time. She had to start taking sleeping-pills, and then pills to kill the pain. She would get so dopey that she had to take still more pills to wake her up again. The trouble with these things is that their effect is cumulative, and she started to depend on these drugs to keep normal. On three or four occasions she took too many of them and I had to get doctors in with a stomach pump to wake her up again. It was all most sad and distressing.

It had been a very happy marriage. I never ceased to be in love with her, but the difference in our ages caught up with us, at least on her side. She felt that she was getting older and that the danger existed of my running off with someone else some day. In fact nothing could have been further from my mind. I had never looked at another woman since the day we married. But, in retrospect, I do think it is a bad mistake for two people of such widely differing ages to marry, and it is much harder for a woman. She feels she is losing her looks and losing her physical charms, which may not necessarily be what you married her for.

To try a change of air and new surroundings we had gone, in August 1945, to spend a few weeks at the Beech Hill Private Hotel at Rushlake Green in Sussex. It was run by Mrs. Tito Wessel, a marvellous person of whom I shall have more stories to tell. Her husband, from whom she was divorced, was a Dane who had been isolated in his own country by the war. She suddenly found herself with no money at all, and had turned her house in the country into a

155

private hotel. She made us wonderfully comfortable and did everything she possibly could for Clare.

It was on the evening of 1 September that the tragedy occurred. I had spent most of the day in bed as my younger son had kicked me very hard in a very painful spot, and the doctor had said I ought to rest up for twenty-four hours to give the swelling a chance to go down. Clare came in from the other bedroom early in the evening to say that she was in bad pain and feeling very tired. We had a lovely golden Labrador at the time. The dog had been unwell for three or four days and my wife had stayed up most of the night looking after it. She was obviously distraught and miserable, and at the end of her tether.

The cook, with whom we had made friends, sent me up a very nice dinner on a tray. She had gone to a lot of trouble when rationing was at its worst, and had somehow gathered together all sorts of appetizing bits and pieces. When Clare saw it she became rather hysterically cross and said that I must send it down again and say the food was disgusting. The trouble was that she had become terribly jealous and possessive about me. She could not bear any attention being centred on me and wanted to be the main object of attraction to everybody round her, as she had been all her life.

We had one of those silly arguments people have when they are tired and overwrought: 'Don't be stupid,' I said. 'It all looks very nice and they have taken a lot of trouble.'

'Either you like them more than me, or you send it down and say it is disgusting,' she snapped back.

'It's got nothing to do with my feelings for you, what's on this tray.'

'Oh! obviously you like them better than me,' she went on and flounced back into her own bedroom.

Then she mixed herself a stiff dry martini and said she was going to take as many pills as she felt would make her sleep. By now she was crying and hysterical and I heard her open the drawer of her bedside table, rustling with the envelope where she kept the capsules. 'I must sleep; I will take as many of these as I like,' I heard her saying.

156

I thought I had better stop her doing anything stupid, so I got out of bed and went into the next room. The envelope with the sodium amytal tablets was empty. She was already getting drowsy, but I shook her and asked her how many she had taken. 'About forty,' she mumbled.

This was serious. She usually took her pills with water, but I knew they would act much more quickly after the strong martini she had mixed. I rushed into the bathroom, made a stiff mixture of salt and water and forced her to swallow it. Then I telephoned frantically for a doctor. By the time he arrived with his stomach pump it was too late. She was dead.

Of course it meant all the horrible business of a coroner's inquest, at which I had to tell the whole story of her illness and the last scene we had had. 'Has there been any prior occasion when she has taken these tablets and spat them out?' the coroner asked me. I had to admit that there was. 'On several occasions?'—'Quite a number. I think to frighten me.'

'In what way to frighten you?'—'She wanted me to be more sympathetic, more understanding, I think. She used to get so frightfully overwrought and I thought the only way to help her was to try to be firm. She would never take them intentionally to do away with herself. After these occasions she has always said: "I would never do away with myself"—actually for the children's sake.'

'Your suggestion is that owing to her being so extremely overwrought she was reckless?' the coroner went on. 'I am certain of it. She loved her children and was far too devoted a mother. She would never have contemplated it; she was frightened of that. She loved life and was always doing anything she could to help people.'

He returned an open verdict, and I was left with my two small sons, alone again.

CHAPTER NINE

WARM AT LAST

IF it had not been for Denise Wessel I do not know what I would have done after my wife died. After the war she married again, becoming the wife of the Duke of Leinster, and she is now my mother-in-law. She is one of the most enchanting and fabulous characters I have ever met. Her maiden name was Jessie Smithers and she is the daughter of a judge's clerk. She went on the stage in the days of George Edwardes, changed her name to Denise Orme and became one of the main attractions at Daly's and the Alhambra, Leicester Square, where it is said that she used to sing a song called 'No One Ever Marries Me'. However, her first marriage was to Lord Churston, by whom she had four daughters, who were well known as society beauties between the two wars as the Yarde-Buller girls. The eldest, Joan, was married to Loel Guinness before she became the first wife of Aly Khan. Denise became Lady Ebury and Primrose became Lady Cadogan. The third daughter, Lydia, married Captain Ian de Hoghton Lyle, who was killed during the war. She paid a brief visit with her two children to her mother's house-cum-hotel, while I was staying there with Clare, and then left to spend the autumn with her mother-in-law up in Scotland.

Beech Hill always had a floating population of family, with daughters, sons and grandchildren always centring on their mother's and grandmother's house, in addition to the paying guests. I received a lasting impression of a large devoted family with a tremendous consciousness and love of each other, and used to think what a contrast it was to my own childhood.

Denise Wessel was the hub of the whole thing. She loves

158

entertaining, loves people and has never really quite left the stage. She must have an audience; even if the audience consists of bores it doesn't really make much difference, although once she is bored with people, she has an absolute genius for getting rid of them. People will be firmly ensconced in their chairs and she will suddenly rise to her feet, shake them by the hand and say, 'I'm so sorry you're going. Do come again,' pull them out of their chairs and push them backwards out of the room. At the same time this is combined with a tremendously hospitable nature. She asks people for lunch or dinner and then completely and utterly forgets all about them. They turn up quite unexpectedly just as you are finishing lunch or dinner yourself, and you have to start the meal all over again, trying to spin out the food that has just been cleared.

With her tremendously grand manner you would think she was the daughter of the Lord Chief Justice himself. She looks frightfully vague, but the first thing she does in the morning is to pick up *The Financial Times* and juggle with the stocks and shares with fantastic insight. Over the years she has made a lot of money from investments and from buying houses and selling them, and is an incredible judge of what will prove a profitable deal. Generous to a fault with all her family, to whom she would give anything in the world, if the butcher or baker slip an extra threepence on the bill she is down on them in a minute.

I left Beech Hill reluctantly to return to London and open up the empty house in Wilton Street. I got in a nanny to look after the two little boys and found myself being welcomed by all the people who had so blatantly cold-shouldered me after my first marriage. I cannot say that their attitude on either occasion improved them in my estimation, but I found life became much more pleasant after I met Lydia Lyle again. She had taken a house in St. John's Wood, and in due course we started to see a lot of each other. We both had the same problems, both of us had lost our spouses, both of us had two children to look after and found each other's company very congenial.

My chief preoccupation at the time was to get myself another job. I had not really regained any contact with my father, and my financial difficulties remained the same, with the problem of at least one boy who would soon be of prep school age. Through Lydia Lyle I had met her brother-in-law, Aly Khan, who invited me to go out to India with him to see his father, the Aga Khan, weighed in diamonds on the occasion of his jubilee. It was the most glorious holiday I have ever spent. For the first time in my life I was conscious of being warmed through to the bone, something that, with the experience of my father's and mother's houses and our little cottage at Reading, not to mention the drill hall at Caterham, I had never assumed to be possible.

This was still pre-partition India, and it was like something out of *The Arabian Nights*. Straight from rationed England I found myself in a world of maharajahs and fifty-foot-long tables groaning with food. The Aga Khan had an extraordinary house in Bombay which, as far as I could see, was a small town of bungalow houses, all joined together next to one another. Some were very old and there was a fantastic conglomeration of furniture dating from the different periods when the various sections had been built. I always remember the rats that used to come up the waste-pipe in the bathroom and eat the soap. You had to hide it in a cupboard if you wanted anything to wash with in the morning.

Later on—the details are a blur—I stayed at another house of his which was a complete Victorian survival, with box hedges and a garden laid out in symmetrical patterns, something very extraordinary to find in the middle of this tropical continent. The Aga was a fascinating old gentleman, a very big person indeed and a very fine character. I was tremendously impressed with all the good works and charitable organizations with which he was connected. In England one had only known him as a society figure with a racing stable and it was very refreshing to see all the hospitals his family supported, and the educational facilities they provided. All the money that was given for the buying and weighing of the diamonds was returned for charitable services all over India.

While I was there, Aly Khan introduced me to the wealthy Mungee family, who were planning to set up a series of chain stores in India and wanted to found an import-export subsidiary in London to provide them with the necessary goods. When I got back I was appointed a working director at their office in Curzon Street, so I was busy and more or less solvent again.

My father had in the meantime returned from Scotland and was making preparations for setting up residence again at Woburn. The government people had left the place in an absolute shambles, and he had decided that much reconstruction work had to be done before it could be lived in again. He asked Professor Albert Richardson to draw up plans which included demolishing the entire east wing, which was so riddled with dry rot that it had become uninhabitable. While preparations for this work were going on, my father settled in one of his own houses in the village. He never was to live at the Abbey as Duke of Bedford.

I was seeing him again from time to time and used to try to discuss with him the ramifications of the estate and what the problems were. I begged him to let me have one of the houses in the village so that I could start acquiring some sense of my future responsibilities, but I was brushed off every time. He always had some excuse ready about no house being available or the time not being ripe, and after this sort of thing happens ten or a dozen times, you begin to cotton on to the fact that you are not wanted around.

My brother, who is about five years younger than I am, and was by then in his middle twenties, had been properly trained in estate management, and it was perfectly clear that my father preferred to have him entrusted with the matter. I hardly know my brother at all. I remember him as a boy who used to inherit my successive tutors after they had given me up as a bad job, but from the time I was seventeen and he was twelve, I seldom saw him. I think my father found him very much easier to get on with than I was and he had certainly taken greater pains to conform to my father's eccentricities and educational whims than I ever had.

My sister, who is three years younger than I am, has never married and leads a completely separate life with a woman friend. Her *ménage* is an odd symposium of all our family traits, with dogs' messes on the carpets contrasting with Cartier pieces, and jeroboams of brandy, standing on oilcloth-covered tables. I am too much of a sybarite not to like everything perfect and although we get on quite well we see very little of each other. My mother had faded out of my life completely after my marriage to Clare and, although after twenty years we have started exchanging Christmas presents again, there is practically no contact at all.

Not long after I returned from India, Lydia and I realized that we were in love. On 12 February 1947 we announced our engagement and, in order to keep the ceremony as quiet as possible, we married the same day. This match was very much more to my father's liking and, rather to my surprise, he gave us one of the houses on the Chenies estate to live in. It was quite a handsome old Georgian house and we were delighted. It had a little lodge cottage into which we moved with the children while we drew up various plans to have it modernized and converted. However, this was the time when not only were materials short and you needed planning permission and building licences for everything you did, but the surveyor very soon discovered that the whole structure was riddled with dry rot. The only thing to do was to pull the whole place down—it would have fallen down anyway within five years—and we were left with nowhere to provide a home for the children. Neither of us particularly fancied the idea of bringing them up in London. We wanted them to live natural, open-air lives and have a healthy, normal education. London would have been much too expensive and we cudgelled our brains as to what to do next.

We both had some money coming in and worked out

that, if I sold the house in Wilton Street and Lydia sold her house in St. John's Wood, we would have enough capital to move right out of England and make a new start. If we could find somewhere with lower taxation this would pay for the education of the children. I had come back so exhilarated with the heat and warmth of India that I was prepared to go almost anywhere to escape the cold and damp of England. My work with the Mungee representation was going quite well, but I was prepared to sacrifice even that if we could set up a really happy home where we could feel the sun on our backs.

More or less on the spur of the moment, without making any real preparation or enquiry, we decided to emigrate to South Africa, buy a farm and run it as a commercial proposition. I have never seen my father so pleased as he was when I told him what we intended. He became positively mellow and came to see us all off on the 'plane on 1 March 1948, beaming with smiles, and patting me on the back. He was pleasant and friendly and charming for the first time in my whole life. I can only suppose he was glad to see the back of me.

The journey out and our arrival at Johannesburg were a disaster and we would not have needed very much persuasion to turn round and come right back home again. Air travel was still being run more or less on a war-time basis and it had taken weeks to organize the flight, which involved our changing in Lisbon. We had a vast collection of luggage with us, some of it tied up with string, and when we landed the Portuguese customs undid absolutely everything, strewing the contents everywhere. When all this had been put together again, the passengers were dispersed to various hotels, but none of the right luggage accompanied them. My wife had an airman's uniforms and an airman had my wife's hats. At our hotel the children were somewhere up on the tenth floor of a modern annexe and we were down in an awful old barn of a palace, with one dim bulb hanging in the centre of a vast room. In trying to sort things out, I stumbled over something while carrying my wife's jewel-case and came down with such a whack that everything fell out all over the floor. We spent an hour or more in the semi-dark crawling round with a lighter picking up her various baubles.

The next morning passengers and luggage were more or less reunited; everything was opened again by the customs, in spite of the fact that we had had no contact with our belongings at all. We then flew through a series of terrible electric storms, with the 'plane getting bogged down at unlikely places like Accra and Leopoldville. When we arrived at Johannesburg, expecting to find warm weather, we were greeted by a bitter hailstorm and freezing, biting wind. We had sent all our winter clothes by sea and only had tropical things with us, so the first thing we had to do was to go out and buy winter clothes for everybody, the cold was so terrible. That shattered our first illusions.

After a short rest, we took the train to the Cape. Now apart from the trans-Siberian Express, this is the dreariest journey in the world. For the best part of a couple of days the scenery never changes. It is flat, waterless, featureless plateau, baked brown and stretching to the horizon in every direction. Our pockets were stuffed with particulars of farms with avenues of old oaks, houses with old Dutch gables, and streams running through the grounds, and all we could see was this arid desert. Our hearts sank, Lydia, who hates any countryside that doesn't look green, was appalled. It is only about a hundred miles before Cape Town that the scenery takes on a human aspect. The change is quite extraordinary. The train drops down through wooded hills which look half like Cornwall and half like Surrey.

A good friend had undertaken to look after us and the children during the initial stages, and we spent weeks, driving hundreds and hundreds of miles, trying to find our dream farm. It was nearly four months before we decided on a 200-acre fruit and vineyard estate called Waterfall in the Drakenstein Mountains, about forty miles from Cape Town. It is a lovely part of the world. There is a big waterfall, as the name suggests, tumbling down the mountains at the back, and although the house was a pretty hideous shack with no electric light, we made up our minds that we could convert it into the sort of thing we wanted.

Over the years we have turned it into a sort of American Colonial-style house with plenty of bathrooms. It really is a dream place, and now that we live in England I often long to go back there. We gradually turned the land into a going concern. The vineyards were rotten, so I pulled them all up, planting apricots and olives and a strange herb called *buchu*, which has valuable medicinal properties and is exported mostly to America. The only trouble is that its price fluctuates rather alarmingly.

I certainly look back on the South African period as the happiest time in my life. It was a fairly simple existence, we worked quite hard, but we had enough money coming in, and we made many friends. It was wonderful for the children, who learned to ride, spent most of the daylight hours out of doors and fairly blossomed with health. For the first time I came to realize the joys of really happy family life, and now that I have less time and more responsibilities, I look back on these years with real nostalgia.

There is no doubt that if you can ignore the local politics, it is an almost idyllic part of the world in which to live. In Johannesburg money is the only really important thing and everything revolves around it. But down in Cape Province the pace of life is much slower. There are a great many charming people with some lovely houses and beautiful furniture, and we made and still maintain a lot of good friends. I had built a swimming-pool, we used to play a lot of golf and life was very pleasant and easy.

Somebody said to me not so long ago that it is a wonderful country to live in as long as you don't think, and I am afraid this is true. Even living our relatively isolated farm and country life, the colour-conscious atmosphere and the politics start to weigh you down. The *Afrikaners* have never forgotten the Boer War. It is as if it happened five years ago, so strong is the memory in their minds. They talk about British concentration camps as if they were Dachau and Belsen, and make up stories about their grandmothers having been fed on glass. I believe in actual fact that this was isinglass, which is the stuff from which you make jelly for soup. Their minds are quite closed to all argument, and unless you have been born in the country it is very difficult to understand their prejudices.

The native and coloured populations live in the most ghastly conditions, with no sanitation, and their dwellings literally strung together out of paper and old squashed petrol tins. The problem is so big that you do not know how to tackle it as an individual, particularly if you are not of the country. I often wanted to take some active part, but conditions are such that even their own members of parliament, if they do not do what the government likes, or if it is thought that they are going to go out of South Africa and criticize it in some way, are refused a passport to leave. It is an appalling state of affairs, which got worse the whole time we were there, ever since the death of Marshal Smuts. You have this marvellous country-side and glorious climate, the most tremendous potentialities for development, very good friends, but there is no avoiding the fact that conditions leave a bitter taste in your mouth.

We used to get back to England about once every two years and gorged ourselves on theatre and ballet and all the metropolitan pleasures you miss, in spite of the sun. Relations with my father grew almost cordial now that we were six thousand miles away most of the time. We used to exchange quite civil letters, and a couple of years after we had arrived there he settled a certain amount of money on me as part of the provisions he was making to protect the Bedford estates from the incidence of death duties and taxation. It made a great difference to our existence and for the first time in my life we were really comfortable. Certain capital sums had been put in my name, from which I drew the income, but as events turned out, he had done it just too late to keep the estate intact when he died.

From odd press cuttings and letters, I learnt that he was taking up his political activities again. The British People's Party had been resurrected after the war, with John Beckett again appointed as its secretary, but its attempt to hold public meetings received short shrift. On two occasions their meetings were broken up by hecklers shouting anti-Fascist slogans and telling my father to 'go back to Germany', and I think even he realized there was no headway to be made against established public opinion.

Anyone who wrote a letter to the newspapers of which he approved used to receive by the first post next morning a fat envelope full of my father's pamphlets, accompanied by a brief personal note. His industry in these blind alleys continued to be quite extraordinary. He went on writing his letters to any newspaper who would print them, about financial policy, or, more harmlessly, on the behaviour of birds and animals, on the subject of which he was at least an expert. I remember he took part in one very odd experiment shortly after we had left for South Africa, when he was one of a group of people helping Dr. Hugh Cott, the Cambridge scientist, to test a theory that brightly coloured birds are unpalatable, by eating tawny owls, a cockatoo, a greenfinch and a cormorant.

One thing he knew nothing about was pictures, and I was horrified in 1951 to receive a catalogue, after the sale was over, of over two hundred paintings from the Woburn collection, which he had sent to be auctioned, either because he thought they were of relatively little interest, or because there was nowhere to hang them now that the east wing of the house had gone. They only realized just over twenty-seven thousand pounds and they included a Cuyp, a Murillo and a Ruysdael, which attracted the top price of two thousand, five hundred guineas. I wrote off frantic letters saying I hoped that nothing of family interest had been disposed of and he assured me that I had nothing to fear. He had had my brother and an expert in to vet the canvases, but their knowledge of family history was not what it should have been, and some of the more interesting minor portraits have gone for ever. The picture of the Lord Southampton, whose daughter brought Bloomsbury into the family, was sold for about fifty pounds. If I had known I would have bought it myself, but now it is too late.

During 1951 I also read in the papers that part of our Bloomsbury property had been sold for £1,620,000, chiefly for the purpose of paying off death duties on my grandfather's estate. By now the Bedford holdings which had survived into the nineteenth century had been much diminished. The land round Tavistock, Chenies and Woburn was still more or less intact, but all our London properties, apart from some of Bloomsbury, had by now gone.

The reconstruction work at Woburn also got him into trouble. In March 1953 a summons was issued for overspending and building without a licence. Mrs. Samuel, who had remained as his general factotum, and a Mr. W. Cunningham, a London surveyor, were sent for trial on the charges. In the end she was fined fifty pounds, and Mr. Cunningham was ordered to pay a hundred pounds costs, while the London and Devon Estates Company, the family company in which all our properties had been vested since the time of my grandfather, was fined five thousand pounds with three hundred pounds costs.

From the tip of South Africa, all this seemed to be happening on another planet. My father made no attempt to keep me informed of what he was doing with our family possessions, and I had more or less resigned myself to the situation and began to feel more and more as if I had been bought out of the family. It was no good complaining. We were very happy and comfortable on our South African farm and when Lydia gave birth to our son Francis in 1950, he finally completed our three-cornered brood of children. The long years of unpleasantness with my father and grandfather started to fade into the background, and we assumed that the pattern of our lives was set for decades to come.

I was out playing golf on the links at Paarl during the

second week of October in 1953 when I was called to the telephone at the club-house. It was a newspaper reporter who said that a message had just come through from England that my father was missing. I told him the story was ridiculous. My father never went anywhere to be missing. He never travelled and was always surrounded by his staff and servants, either at Woburn, Endsleigh or in Scotland, and the question of his being 'missing' simply could not arise. I went back rather crossly to my interrupted round.

We had only played a few more holes when I was fetched to the club-house again for another call, this time from a newspaperman I knew. His version was that my father was missing over some water. This I knew to be even more unlikely as, apart from his trip to Ireland during the war, he had never gone abroad during my lifetime. I told my journalist friend that there must be some mistake and that if he checked back he would find the whole story was without foundation. I finished our much interrupted game, changed, went into the bar and was just enjoying a cool glass of beer when the telephone bell rang again.

This time it was a newspaper in London who had got the golf-club number from my home. I knew from my experience in Fleet Street that newspapers do not encourage telephone calls to the other side of the world unless they are in possession of pretty hard information. Their news was that my father was missing down at his Endsleigh estate in the West Country. I was quite unable to help them in any way, but began to think that something serious must have occurred. When I got back home I told Lydia that it looked as if I would have to fly back to London to find out what had happened. She said, very sensibly, that if there were any truth in the story I would have heard something from the family, which put me in two minds again, but it was not long before my brother himself was on the line. He confirmed that my father was indeed missing and that we must expect the worst. I was completely dazed by this and cudgelled my brain as to what could have happened. There must have been an accident of some sort, I felt, as any idea of my father dying so soon had simply never entered my head. He was a very abstemious man who never smoked and never drank and there seemed no reason why he should not live into his nineties.

I was obviously no use six thousand miles away, so I persuaded the airline people to accept an emergency booking, and the next day started the long flight back to London. I had no sooner got out for the stop-over at Johannesburg when the newspaper people were on to me with the news that my father had been found shot dead in the park at Endsleigh. I was travelling alone, there was no one for me to turn to, and I felt completely bewildered. My father had been an accomplished game shot since his early childhood and it seemed to me quite incredible that a man with that much experience could have had an accident with a gun.

Slowly the bemused realization came to me that I had become the Duke of Bedford. It was a terrible shock. I felt completely unprepared to accept the new responsibilities entailed. I had never been allowed to learn anything about the situation or workings of the estate, or even what provisions for its management and disposal my father had made. I knew a sudden death like this had completely wrecked the finances of other families in our position, and arrived in London fearing the worst.

I was met by Lydia's two sisters, Joan Aly Khan and Primrose Cadogan. I took the night train down to Devon and the following morning was at Endsleigh. The inquest had been held the day before and the cremation service had already taken place.

Endsleigh is a hideous Victorian house standing in the middle of our Tavistock estates. The position is beautiful, with the land sloping down to the river Tamar, surrounded by lovely old trees and wonderful scenery. I think it was probably my grandfather's favourite property. He had a lot of landscape gardening done, and when the local lead mines closed down he arranged for some of the miners to come and dig a vast water garden so that they should not be unemployed. He improved the fishing, and bought up the banks of the river for miles so that their breeding grounds should not be interfered with in any way. I suspect a number of people took advantage of this, and sold their stretches of the bank at prices way above what they were worth, but he made it into one of the finest salmon and trout streams in England. My father had turned part of the house into a boarding-house under Mrs. Samuel, to accommodate twenty-five or thirty guests, who were charged twelve guineas a week.

The place was full of women. My mother had turned up, unexpectedly transformed into an enthusiastic widow. Mrs. Samuel, needless to state, was there in force. There was a Miss Dix who had been one of my father's secretaries, and half a dozen other females who had been connected with his various pamphleteering enterprises, or received pensions of some sort from him.

It was as much as I could do to obtain a coherent account of what had really happened. Apparently my father had gone out about seven o'clock in the morning on Friday, 9 October with his gun to shoot hawks or cormorants, as was his usual practice. When he did not return for lunch, the estate people started looking for him, and by the following morning a full-scale search had been organized. The estate people were joined by police and a hundred Royal Marines and Commandos from Beckley, near Plymouth, with walkie-talkie apparatus, but of course with thousands of acres to search he might have been anywhere. They were on the point of dragging the river Tamar when his body was found by two estate workers in some undergrowth off a small private drive not five hundred yards from the house. He had died instantaneously from a gunshot wound in the head.

The verdict was accidental death. Like so many of his ancestors, my father's sight had been failing for some time, and it may be that he stumbled, although what an experienced shot could have been doing going round through undergrowth with his gun cocked and loaded instead of broken is, I must confess, beyond me. There are certainly those who think it was not an accident. My father had become very depressed during the last months of his life. One or two of the people nearer to him than I had ever been had gained the impression of a completely disillusioned man. All his political, social, and religious notions had led him nowhere, causing only derision and antipathy in the public mind.

I think he realized that several of his sycophantic associates had just been battening on him as a source of income and had not sincerely shared his opinions at all. One or two of them, who will have to be nameless, had done very well out of him. Above all, he had found no one in his life to give him the affection I am sure he craved. In spite of his high-flown, abstract ideas of brotherly love, he had been totally incapable of exhibiting affection himself on a person-to-person basis, and towards the end he was a lonely and rather desolate man.

His death had caused chaos in the estate. If he had lived until the end of the year, various provisions he had made for disposing of the different properties, such as the settlements he had made on me, and others, would have met the necessary legal requirements, and thus escaped estate duty. As it was, his unsettled estate, valued at £802,252, and the settled lands valued at £7,800,000 qualified for something like four and a half million pounds of tax, which is the mess in which we find ourselves to-day. My father had drawn up no final directions for the conduct of the estate, and the whole problem was, therefore, dumped back into the hands of the trustees. All I could think of was what was going to happen to Woburn and what I was going to have to do to keep this historic old house in the family.

CHAPTER TEN

SÈVRES IN THE SINK

M Y first visit to Woburn in thirteen years was a shattering experience. I had not been there since my grandfather's death and no member of the family had lived there in all that time. When my father returned from Scotland after the war he lived in one of the houses in the village, while the reconstruction work he had ordered was put in train. As the long drive from the lodge gates curved round the last wooded hillock I gasped. The Abbey looked as if a bomb had fallen on it. The building which had housed the indoor riding-school and the tennis court, connecting the two Flitcroft stable blocks, had disappeared; so had the whole of the east front, together with at least a third of the north and south wings where it had joined them. There were piles of stones and building materials lying in a haphazard fashion all over the place, and the courtyard in the centre of the house was full of Nissen huts. There were one or two workmen around, but otherwise the place was deserted. A troop of Alsatian dogs, chained to long wires, kept watch at most of the gates, and you could hear them barking and their chains rattling like some eerie scene out of *The Hound of the Baskervilles*.

The interior was freezing-cold and desolate. It looked as if it belonged to a series of bankrupt auction rooms. There were piles and piles of linen baskets in the front hall, right up to the ceiling, and mounds of furniture lying everywhere, most of it without dust sheets. There were beautiful Louis XV chairs with kitchen-table legs straight through the seat; the walls and cornices were peeling and everything was covered in dust, and filthy. The whole house reeked of damp. It looked as if no general maintenance work had been done at all. I do not think my father had paid any attention whatsoever to the details of upkeep, and after one quick tour I despaired of ever breathing life into the place again.

I spent a day or two at my father's house in the village, trying to gather together the threads of what would have to be done, but the shambles at the Abbey was nothing compared with the chaos into which the whole Bedford estate had been thrown by my father's untimely death. The house in the village was infinitely depressing with a nasty jumble of furniture arranged with no taste at all. There was a strong smell of disinfectant everywhere. My father had always had a mortal fear of germs, and used to carry a huge bottle of T.C.P. tablets around in his pocket—if anyone ever coughed or sneezed he immediately sucked a lozenge. The whole house had been sprayed with some sort of germ-killer. Mrs. Samuel was very much in evidence, extremely grand in a large car with a chauffeur. I realized that if anyone could help me with the details of what running the Abbey involved, she would be the person, but our old antagonism of the thirties proved too strong for me to feel like taking her into my confidence. I had also been very conscious of the position in which I had been placed during my first marriage, when Mrs. Samuel, as the resident caretaker of Woburn, used to send us occasional hampers of food as a form of largesse. Now I could not bring myself to warm to her, or invite her assistance.

I soon escaped to London again for a series of sessions with the trustees. It is only fair to say that they had been put in an impossible position. It looked as if the whole estate would have to be mortgaged to pay off the death duties, and until some reasonable assessment had been made of our liabilities, it was hopeless to make any plans for the future. As far as we could make out, there were no specific instructions which would prevent me taking the first place in the family, but as everything concerning the property and the inheritance was left entirely to their discretion, it was no good trying to rush things. I realized that I would have to leave them to their appalling task and somehow gain their confidence. They were all very much older than I was, completely bound by the terms of the trust, and they made it gently but firmly clear that they had the power to do exactly as they saw fit.

The only pleasant surprise I had was when I asked if there was any family jewellery included in the estate. My grandmother had worn very little during the three or four years I had known her and my mother, poor woman, had been lucky to have a dress during most of her marriage, much less a brooch or any finery. A few cousins had remembered that my great-grandmother had usually been decked out in true Victorian style, but they did not think that there would be very much left. I went along with the family solicitor to a safe deposit in a London bank and we discovered a most tremendous cache. There was a fabulous diamond necklace I had never seen, three or four tiaras, one of them with the flower design picked out in diamonds, and a whole collection of other necklaces. They were all heirlooms of course and only added to the tax liability. There seemed little likelihood at the time that we would be able to keep any of them.

I realized that there was nothing useful I could do for the time being, so I decided to return to South Africa while things sorted themselves out again. Lydia was clamouring to have me back, and from what I had been able to learn it looked as if the thirteenth Duke of Bedford was going to have to end his days as a fruit farmer in South Africa. As it was, we went on growing *buchu* herbs and apricots for several months while we waited for some indication from the trustees of the course events would take. The money aspect of it all left me relatively cold. Of course it is nice to be really comfortably off, but when you have had to live on ninety-eight pounds a year, all talk of millions becomes completely unreal. News filtered in from London which made it look as if something might be salvaged from the wreck, but although there would be a substantial income, in modern terms, available to the family, there seemed to be no way of devising any arrangement which would permit the refur-

175

bishing and upkeep of Woburn, which to me was the only object worth preserving in the whole estate.

I could not have cared less what happened to Bloomsbury or Tavistock, but I felt that if Woburn was sold or otherwise disposed of to the National Trust or some institution, something would have gone out of the family, and indeed the history of England, which could never possibly be replaced. Unless it could be restored in its proper form, I saw no point in going back to England just to live off the money, and as I was in no position to make my views prevail, we decided at one juncture to stay where we were and let the whole problem look after itself.

I felt I should perhaps take some advice in the matter, so I wrote to Max Beaverbrook. He is one of those people whom you may not see for five years, yet the contact remains as warm and friendly as if you met him every day. I asked him if he thought there was any point in my coming back from South Africa. What with death duties and the inability to carry out one's responsibilities, it seemed to me that there was no future for the aristocracy in England. I told him that I felt we belonged to the past, and that I would sooner stay in a part of the world which was young and growing and vital. I must say his answer was the last one I expected. Very sharply and tersely he told me in effect: Come back and get on with the job you are supposed to do as Duke of Bedford.

With many forebodings, Lydia and I decided to follow this advice, although it would break our hearts to leave Waterfall. However, I had found myself making several strong comments about the South African Government's *apartheid* policy, one or two of which had been reported in the Cape Town newspapers, and we thought it might be a good idea to pay at least a short visit to England while ruffled tempers calmed down.

We came back by ship this time, with the family, and arrived at Plymouth in the late spring of 1954. We spent a week or ten days at Endsleigh, which had reverted to being a hotel. The ghillies were most insistent that I should taste the fruits of their labour, so I finally succumbed to pressure and went out with a fishing-rod on the banks of the Tamar. Within twenty minutes, for the first time in my life, I caught the most enormous salmon, and in some curious symbolic way, the excitement of it wiped out at one fell swoop a whole host of unpleasant childhood memories of trudging through fished-out pools behind my father. I began to think there must be something in this duke business after all.

The first step was to find somewhere to live. My mother-in-law had bought herself a house in Jersey, and was waxing so lyrical about the income-tax savings this permitted, that we decided to follow suit. At least it would serve as a base while we really decided what was to be done about Woburn. We had a session with the trustees, and asked if we could go down and make a corner of it habitable in order to study the problem. They rather shrugged their shoulders and said we were perfectly free to do so if we saw fit, but that my father and Professor Richardson had removed the whole kitchen block, and that there was nowhere even to cook. However, we said we would eat out at the Bedford Arms in the village if necessary, so a few rooms were hurriedly whitewashed and put in order; brass-knobbed beds were put into the bedrooms so that we could camp during our short visits. The place was still in utter chaos; none of the rest of the house had been touched, and we very nearly abandoned the proposition of getting it into working order before we started.

I had realized from the beginning that the only way of financing the reopening of the house would be to follow the tentative example of other families in our position, and allow the public to see it in return for an entrance fee. The trustees had distinct reservations about the whole idea. They said that however attractive we made it, we would be lucky to earn enough to meet the outgoings. To me the whole future of the family, and indeed its right to exist in the second half of the twentieth century, was bound up with the reopening of Woburn. In so far as I am able to concentrate on anything, it became an obsession with me. Thanks to my kind cousins in the thirties I had developed a real interest in the history and traditions of my family. I wanted to try to live up to them, to carry on the development of the estates, make them more prosperous, do my duty to the county in the way of going on committees and opening bazaars and laying foundation stones, in fact doing all the things which I was designed for, or at least was meant to do. I had always respected the manner in which my grandfather had attended to the details of administering the estate and I wanted to do the same thing, but in a more human and friendly way.

I had never actually seen this business of opening stately homes to the public in operation. This was probably a good thing, as otherwise I would have done it the same way as other people did, and made no more of a success of it than most of the others. I did go to see Sir Owen Morshead, the librarian at Windsor, who gave me a number of tips on how to handle the presentation of the historical side of it. In the end I also paid a couple of incognito visits to other houses open to the public. However, they were all doing it rather on the theory that the sooner the visitors were in the sooner they would be gone and the quicker you got the money the better and good-bye.

That was not the way I intended to do it. I wanted to make people enjoy themselves, give them service and value for money and make sure they would come back again. If this enabled me to live in my ancestral home, then everyone would be satisfied. We had these five children, all of whom we loved deeply, and I wanted to give them somewhere to live where we could all be amused and enjoy ourselves, a place where every member and generation of the family could have something which gave them a central point of attraction in their lives.

We made up our minds that we would make part of the house attractive to visitors and then, if the money started coming in, we would make part of one wing habitable for ourselves. The question was where to start. There were no indoor servants left. Mrs. Samuel had pensioned the last of them off, although there were night-watchmen and labourers and carpenters on the building staff of the estate office, on whose services we could occasionally call. When they realized that we meant seriously to restore the house to its former glory, they became positively enthusiastic and put in hours and hours of overtime just to help us, but in the initial stages it just meant my wife and I and the couple of servants we had brought with us, wearing our oldest clothes, rolling up our sleeves and getting to grips with this Herculean task.

One advantage was that we were starting from scratch. The east wing, where all the guest suites had been, had gone, and the furniture from them was piled up in the other rooms of the house. All the furniture and hangings from the two Belgrave Square houses had also been dumped there, or in various odd rooms round the village. All the important state-rooms in the Inigo Jones north wing and the Flitcroft-Henry Holland conversion of the west and south wings remained intact. There was no one around to say, 'That was not the way grandmother had it.' We were able to build the whole thing up as we went along, cleaning and clearing one room at a time entirely and then somehow, from out of the chaotic jumble in the passages and other rooms, picking the furniture and hangings and pictures which seemed to suit it. By and large I chose the paintings and my wife chose the furnishings. She had much the hardest task and deserves the lion's share of the credit for what was eventually achieved.

We all worked like dogs. Every room was filthy. The gilding was all black, everything had to be washed down and most of it had to be repainted. This, in these lovely old Georgian rooms, meant a professional job, and here the people from the estate had to help as we used no outside labour at all in any of the work. Gradually the wave of filth and decay started to recede. We used to work all day, camping out in this vast house, boiling up water for morning coffee in an electric kettle and then going out to the Bedford Arms in the village for a warm meal in the evening. We would flop into bed dead tired and the next morning we were up early and at it again.

Our own servants were wonderful. My butler, James Boyd, cheerfully turned himself into navvy, furniture remover and general handyman, while producing steaming cups of coffee at welcome intervals from our non-existent kitchen. He had been with the family for years. He started as a footman with my grandfather in Scotland when he was little more than a boy, and then went to work for Baroness d'Erlanger in Venice. He came back to join me in London after the war, moved to South Africa with us, and has remained ever since. He is one of those people who do not mind how many hours a day they work and I do not think we would ever have got through this Augean stable cleansing without him.

Any friends who were unwise enough to come and see how we were getting on were immediately shanghaied as working parties or made to help with the washing-up of the vast collection of filth-encrusted china and glass that kept being turned up in nooks and crannies, not only in the house but in outlying buildings as well. We found the priceless set of Sèvres porcelain, which had been given to the wife of the fourth duke by Louis XV, lying all over the floor in loose boxes in one of the stable blocks. How it had survived the war without damage I cannot imagine.

Lydia and I decided that this was too much responsibility to pass on to anyone else, so we carefully washed it up ourselves, all eight hundred-odd pieces of it. 'For God's sake don't drop anything,' I begged her. And then as I stood at the sink about half-way through the operation there was the most terrible crash behind me. I practically jumped out of my skin, and whipped round only to find her bursting with suppressed laughter at my alarm. She had deliberately picked up a couple of kitchen plates and hurled them on the floor just to make me jump.

We got most of the silver plate sent up from the Bedford office in London. We cleared one of the ground-floor rooms in the north wing, which we now call Mappin & Webb's, to display it, and my mother-in-law and I took the task of hanging it. We were a bit fumble-fingered at first and would put up a wonderful arrangement of a couple of dozen silver vegetable lids, when the whole thing would fall again with the most horrendous clatter, but we got the hang of it in the end.

The worst problem was the paintings. When we arrived, every picture the family possessed was stacked on the floor in the Long Gallery, in rows about twelve feet deep from the wall, with their backs to us. We had no idea what was what, whether it was my great-aunt painted by her sister or whether it was a Van Dyck. We just had to dig away and find out what was there. There were thousands and thousands of prints and a tremendous number of canvases by enthusiastic amateurs who had dabbled in oils. My grandfather's one venture into the arts had been to have copies made in oil of all the dogs depicted in the more important canvases, against a background of their master's or mistress's legs or skirts. Discarding these was the least worry. A numbered catalogue had been drawn up, but as a fair proportion of the entries referred to rooms which no longer existed, it was more of a hindrance than a help.

We did have professional picture-hangers in for the job. Some of the big, heavy Old Masters' canvases were not the sort of thing for amateurs to fool around with. These experts used to turn up every morning and say, 'Well, what do we do now?' So I had to pull myself together and devise a plan to make an artistic entity of each room, which was a very salutary experience. With the history of the house in mind, I found it possible to sort them out into fairly coherent categories, and the only real innovation I introduced was in the corner room on the first floor of the west and south wings. This had been the Canaletto Room for several generations, and although we now used it as our main dining-room, I had always known it as a sitting-room. The fifth duke, it will be remembered, had blocked up the lovely window overlooking the park in order to provide enough wall space for them. I had always been annoyed by this gloomy arrangement, and had the window unblocked again. By careful juggling we managed to get the twenty-one best examples of this unique collection into the same space, although three of them have had to go up one of the staircases. Nowadays it forms part of our private wing of the Abbey, where I must confess we charge an extra shilling for viewing on special days, if only as a small return for all the trouble we took with it.

I cannot say we made any sensational discoveries during the course of the work. Many of the lovely things we found had been half-forgotten, but nothing new in the way of documents bearing on the life of the family came to light. One odd thing was the extraordinary manner in which bits and pieces to do with my grandmother kept turning up all the time. It was very strange how someone who had disliked the house intensely, and had complained of the poor taste of the successive dukes into whose family she had married, managed to leave her imprint so clearly. She had spent as little time as she could at the Abbey and yet her personality came through clearly. Every drawer you opened seemed to be a bit of her: her books and pictures, needle-work, souvenirs, awful drawings of cats and dogs, deer and birds, her bedroom done up in some ghastly kind of modern Chinese lacquer, all of it excessively expensive and particularly nauseating, but quite unmistakable.

Odd and rather touching was all the evidence I found of her interest in me. In spite of those sixteen years when I was utterly unaware of my connexion with the Bedfords, there were press cuttings of my birth and a couple of big volumes full of newspaper excerpts of anything to do with my father's family. There were yellowing pictures out of old *Tatlers*, carefully cut out and pasted in. Clearly the estrangement with his father had not prevented the old lady from preserving an interest in her son and his family.

This sifting and processing was spread over months and was interspersed with long periods in Jersey to put the house we had bought on St. Brelade's Bay in sufficient order for the children to live in. At Woburn we were all huddled into half a dozen rooms up on the bedroom floor without any facilities, and if our efforts to attract people failed, it would be impossible ever to live there. There were also long and laborious sessions with the trustees, trying to get enough money out of them to pay for the capital expenditure involved in new roads in the park and other necessary amenities for our hoped-for flood of guests. The trustees were slowly hiving off part of the family estates to meet the awful burden of taxation. One of the first parcels to go was the 1,681 acres at Chenies, brought into the family by the wife of the first earl four hundred years earlier. It hurt to see these old limbs being lopped off the family tree, but the process was inevitable and there would be far worse to come. I simply had to make a success of my Woburn project or that would go too.

During the winter of 1954 we paid a flying visit to South Africa to collect some of our belongings and find an agent to look after our farm there. On our return to Woburn we found a nice surprise waiting for us. We had a Swiss chef and footman who had joined us from an hotel in Gstaad. They had caught the enthusiasm for work of the older Bedford employees now that there seemed a genuine chance of saving the house for posterity. They had spent untold hours in the Grotto on the ground floor of the Inigo Jones wing, scrubbing the ormer shells and stone stalagmites with nail-brushes and Lux. They must have used fifty packets and the place was transformed. When we left it had been black with the grime of centuries and it was suddenly revealed in all its pastel colours, a sort of water-colour Aladdin's cave. It remains an odd fancy, probably not to everybody's taste, but it is certainly unique.

We had made up our minds to open to the public in April 1955 and the last few weeks were a most appalling rush. There was not only the house but the grounds to get in order. Fortunately the herds of rare animals had good keepers, had been well looked after, and were multiplying. Their conservation had continued during my father's time and he had always paid a certain amount of attention to the upkeep of the park. The new access roads were nearly ready, and most of them had been tarred; sites for car parks had been marked out and two or three of the attractions I had thought of were ready to operate. One of my first ideas had been to have a children's zoo, where they could get to know some of the more attractive and harmless animals, and we also had a playground ready with swings and see-saws, where parents could leave them in good hands while they went on a tour of the park or house. I was also determined to turn at least one of the outside ponds into a boating lake, and the boat-houses and paddle-dinghies were also nearly ready.

We bought the little boats ourselves and rigged up a boat-house to keep them in with a man in charge of them. Catering was another problem. We knew that visitors would clamour for tea, but we quailed at the idea of organizing it ourselves. We decided that the only thing was to convert one of the Flitcroft stable blocks and farm the concession out to a contractor. I was recommended to a firm called Simmons at Hatfield, who have much experience of this sort of thing, and they accepted the offer somewhat grudgingly. They thought it would cause them a lot of work and possible loss, but agreed to pay us ten per cent of their gross receipts. Over the course of the years we have become the biggest part of their business.

Peter Stainer, my father's estate agent, had taken to this revolution in his domain like a duck to water. I think he rather liked the informality of it all and he has become a marvellous publicity agent, always thinking up new attractions to keep us in the public eye. Between us we got a guide-book ready, although I fear we must have driven the printers mad, as we were chopping and changing things around in the house right up to the last moment, and this meant an absolute flood of corrections.

Under our final plan we were able to show all the original state-rooms of the Inigo Jones north wing and the main west front of the house which dates from Flitcroft. The south wing, where Henry Holland did most of his work, was left for some future occasion. This was where we were huddled into our rooms and where we have been able over the course of time to install our private residence.

The loss of the east wing, apart from the exterior, had not really altered the historical character of the original house. It had been made up entirely of suites of bedrooms, sitting-rooms and bathrooms, most of the servants' bedrooms and the kitchens. This was no particular loss, as however successful our venture became, there would never have been any question of returning to eighteenth-century standards and numbers in hospitality. Some of the original Chinese wall-paper had gone, but there is enough left in the north wing to show what it was like.

Lydia had succeeded most cleverly in arranging the main state-rooms for show while still making them look as if they were lived in. She had of course an immense choice of furniture and hangings, as we had never needed to use more than half the vast store of stuff available. She had discarded all the heavy Victorian and Edwardian pieces, banishing the horrible, uncomfortable leather sofas and armchairs I remembered from my grandfather's day, and had concentrated on the French and Georgian pieces. In doing so she completely transformed the house. The heavy, dead atmosphere I recalled from my visits in the thirties had completely gone. It was as if someone had waved a magic wand. It had somehow become a happy house, where people walked round with grins on their faces, instead of sunk in gloom. This is not only a personal reaction. I have found that it affects our visitors the same way. Only I can remember what a miserable place it used to be.

We had plotted out a route for people to follow, and bought miles and miles of rope, and linoleum for them to walk on. Just before the opening day, my wife and I went on our own private conducted tour, trying to see the house as strangers would. We had set out to tell the history of my family in the rooms where a great proportion of it was made. We had worked better than we knew, as over subsequent years we have only had to make minor alterations, and our original plan still stands as we devised it.

Visitors come in on the ground floor at the north-east corner of the Inigo Jones wing, through the former graveyard of the monks to whom the Abbey first belonged. It was turned into a formal garden in the seventeenth century and is now a tree-lined lawn. The first portrait people see in the entrance room is that of Horace Walpole's 'merry little Duke', the fourth one who really gave the house its present form and brought back from his embassy in Paris many of the lovely things we can still show. The room also has one of the few ceilings he had Henry Holland alter in this old north wing. Next door, going west, the ceiling still dates from the Restoration and under it are some of our best books. The Bedfords did not build up very much in the way of a library, but from the fifth duke on, at the end of the eighteenth century, with his passionate and transmitted interest in agricultural affairs and livestock, they made quite a collection of such illustrated books as Redouté's flower books, including his *Jardin de la Malmaison,* Thornton's *The Temple of Flora* and a quite superb copy of John James Audubon's *Birds of America,* which they tell me is probably worth ten thousand pounds or more.

Into the third room along, with the ceiling that Sarah, Duchess of Marlborough so admired, we had put the showcases with the Sèvres china set we had so laboriously washed. I do not suppose we shall ever dare to eat off it and I feel it is rendering a much greater service on display. Its value even in the far-off days when the fourth duke's wife received it from Louis XV was £28,374, and I can well imagine that it is priceless. Only three sets like it were ever made. One is in the Hermitage in Leningrad and the other, much broken and reduced, is in Paris. There is a collection of Sèvres biscuit figures in another display case, and some lovely Meissen services which also date from the second half of the eighteenth century. In our rummaging we had managed to gather together quite a number of pieces of Stourbridge glass and there are two splendid seventeenth-century glass goblets from Ravenscroft's works in London, which we had also found begrimed and filthy out in the stables. Looking down on all this, I hope with approval, is the portrait of Louis XV by Carl van Loo, which he presented to the fourth duke.

Then comes the Grotto, about which I have said enough. It is screened from the garden now by French windows, but unless the weather in England three hundred years ago was very different from our present miserable climate, I cannot possibly fathom what enjoyment was to be derived from sitting in this stone loggia open to the elements on the north side of the house. The park of course would have had the sun full on it, which makes a pretty enough picture, but I still get a fit of the shivers every time I go in there.

The corridor outside these four rooms we still call Paternoster Row, the name which has survived from the old monks who used to walk round the courtyard telling their beads. On the wall I have put some of the portraits of famous people connected with various aspects of the family history. There is a Velazquez of Admiral Adrian Pulido Pareja, who was captain-general of the Armada. A portrait of Robert Devereux, second Earl of Essex, the Elizabethan courtier, and a rather forbidding likeness of Sarah, Duchess of Marlborough, two of whose granddaughters married the third and fourth dukes.

The staircase up to the first floor was redesigned by Henry Holland, and up it, more or less in chronological order, I have hung the portraits of the Earls of Bedford and their wives and families before we became dukes. Henry VIII's first earl is shown in his uniform as Lord High Admiral, the second earl is surrounded by portraits of his children. The third earl has his arm in a sling, which he had to wear more or less permanently as a result of injury, and his wife, Lucy Harington, is dressed in a costume she wore while taking part in a masque by Ben Jonson, performed at the marriage of Robert Carr, Earl of Somerset, and Lady Frances Howard. The wicked countess is shown very appropriately in the most *décolletée* dress I have ever seen. Next come our two splendid Van Dycks, one showing the fourth earl in his Puritan garb. Perhaps he had Inigo Jones build the Grotto as part of his Spartan way of life. The other is of his daughter-in-law, Anne Carr, next to the Lely portrait of her husband, the fifth earl, who became the first duke.

Leading back to the east at the top of the stairs is the Dukes' Corridor, with the portraits of my twelve immediate ancestors and some of their wives. Their artistic merit declines, I fear, in direct proportion to the services the subjects rendered the state, but the Gainsborough portrait of the fourth duke is a good one, showing him with his hand resting on a plan of the Abbey he did so much to rebuild. The ten walnut chairs along the wall date from George II.

At the end on the left is the first of the state-rooms and it is still covered with the Chinese paper imported by the fourth duke in 1755, as fresh to-day as when it was put on. The room has certainly been used as a bedroom in the past, but the Chinese Chippendale chairs and card table were definitely ordered for it and the *famille verte* and *famille rose* Chinese porcelain of the K'anghsi and Chienlung periods were imported in East Indiamen at the same time as the paper.

Into the next room, the only one which we have allowed to retain an unmistakably Victorian air, we have collected together a number of the relics of my grandmother. There is a model of the 'plane in which she made her record flights, some of her travel diaries, some of her own water-colours and *petit point* work, and a number of photographs of her exploits.

The next two rooms in the row, we call the Yellow Drawing-Room and Prince Albert's Dressing-Room. The fourth duke had them refurnished and redecorated in yellow, and the wall-paper is still the original. I felt that the man to whom we really owed our title should have a room to himself, and the main portrait over the chimney-piece in the first of these two rooms is of William, Lord Russell, 'The Martyr', who was executed for his participation in the Rye House Plot in 1683. Under a glass case is the wand he handed to his brother on the scaffold, and the posthumous pardon issued by William and Mary after their accession in 1689. To the left of the chimney is the portrait of his wife, Rachel, who brought us our Bloomsbury properties, and among the other portraits of his immediate family is one of his little sister Anne, who died at the age of five. The interesting thing in this is that she is shown caressing an Australian cockatoo—a hundred and fifty years before Australia was discovered. It must have flown out to sea, landed on an East Indiaman and been brought back as a pet.

The second of these two Yellow Rooms was used by Prince Albert as his dressing-room during his visit to Woburn just after his marriage to Queen Victoria, and we have mounted several of the etchings which the royal pair used to do as a hobby. The founders of the other two titles in the Russell family also have their portraits here. Lord John Russell looks across at the Riesener desk at which he did so much of his work, and opposite him is Lord Odo Russell, brother of the ninth duke and ambassador to Berlin, who was created Baron Ampthill. My wife has also put two of our best pieces of furniture in to keep them company, library tables dating from Louis XV.

The corner room at the end of the wing has always been the State Bedroom. It was occupied by Charles I and Henrietta Maria in 1636, and again by Charles on his visits in 1645 and 1647. Queen Victoria slept there in 1841, and the hangings and coverings on the four-poster bed are still the ones used on that occasion. The sprig of orange blossom from her wedding bouquet is under glass, with the riding-whip she used while at Woburn lying on top. I hope none of the former royal occupants are turning in their graves as a result of putting on the wall the paintings by Sir George Hayter of the trial of William Lord Russell. The ceiling is probably the best in the house, constructed for the fourth duke and copied from a plate in Robert Wand's *Ruins of Baalbeck and Palmyra*. The superb chimney-piece also dates from the eighteenth century, carved by John De Val, who charged a hundred pounds for it even then. This room also gives one of the best views of the park, with the broad drive curving round to the west front, past the lake on which the fourth duke, when he was First Lord of the Admiralty, kept in touch with naval matters by floating a miniature battle-ship.

The rooms across the Flitcroft wing are considerably larger and the first of them, Queen Victoria's Dressing-Room, now has some of our best Dutch and Flemish pictures in it. There is a Cuyp landscape of Nijmegen on the Val, one of the best pictures in the house; another painting of his entitled River Valley with Artist Sketching; a Ruysdael; a Landscape with Figures and Cattle by Berchem; and a sea-scape by Van de Velde. For good measure we have put in the Charles II toilet service of richly embossed silver gilt.

The Blue Drawing-Room next to it is perhaps a misnomer, as all these first three rooms have the same blue damask hangings. This was first put up by the fourth duke but it has been replaced twice since then to the original design. The paintings here are French—among them Claude-Joseph Vernet and Claude Lorrain. The black and gold furniture is also French eighteenth- and nineteenth-century, not not-ably improved by my grandmother's mania for painting most of it white.

The State Saloon in the centre of the wing, with the domed ceiling rising right up to the roof, is the finest room in the house. On the two side walls I have had re-hung two of the five tapestries woven at Mortlake for the fifth earl in 1664 from designs by Raphael depicting the Acts of the Apostles. After the Flitcroft reconstruction they no longer fitted and were moved out into the stables. I have had to leave three in what is now the tapestry tea-room, but two of them at least, the Death of Ananias and the Death of Saphira, have been restored to their proper dignity. One of the best pictures in the room is Murillo's Cherubs Scattering Flowers, and the eighteen-branch chandelier, made in 1758 for eighty-six pounds, is the first one known to have been hung at Woburn.

The last room in the block is the State Dining-Room, which we keep laid out with Sèvres and Stourbridge glass for a dinner-party of twelve, with the Ascot Gold Cup of 1846 in the centre of the table. The equestrian salt cellars come from Versailles and were used at the wedding feast of Louis XV. I have put another Van Dyck of Aubert Lemire, librarian to the Archduke of Austria, over the mantelpiece, but I am afraid that the portraits of Charles I and Henrietta Maria on either side, although attributed to the same artist by former dukes, are only copies.

Behind these state-rooms, looking out on what used to be the inner courtyard but now with a view over to the two stable blocks, is the Long Gallery. This is divided into three bays by four Corinthian columns supporting the roof, and I cannot possibly go into full detail of all the lovely things we have brought together there, or this will start to sound like a catalogue. The only thing is to come and see for yourself. However, as an appetite-whetter, let me say that the first bay contains Holbein's portrait of Henry VIII's third Queen, Jane Seymour, Hans Eworth's portrait of Mary and Philip of Spain, and the great Armada Portrait of Elizabeth I by Gheerhaerts. This has been described and reproduced so often that I hardly need to do so again, but it is a remarkable canvas, showing the Queen in a sumptuous costume encrusted with pearls, the Crown of State by her right arm, her finger pointing on a globe of the world to her newly founded Colony of Virginia. Two little inset scenes in the background show the Armada sailing in bright sunlight up the Channel and the succumbing to the storm on the rocks of Scotland.

In the second bay is the painting of the Battle of Cape La Hogue, won by the Admiral Russell who became Lord Orford, and a portrait of the Duke of Wellington with his aide-de-camp, Lord George William Russell, father of the ninth duke, from whom all of us since are descended. The third bay houses most of the surviving family documents, including the patents of the Garter Knighthoods that have been conferred on nine earls and dukes, ancient family trees and an ebony stick inlaid with mother-of-pearl which belonged to Charles I. He is supposed to have given it to the fourth earl but I rather suspect it was quietly stolen as a souvenir of his visits.

Downstairs at the end of the gallery is the Silver Room, the 'Mappin & Webb's', the Duchess of Leinster and I so laboriously assembled, and a Wardrobe Room which is our local Madame Tussaud's, with wax figures displaying some of the historical family robes.

As we looked at all this, Lydia and I made a great wish that sufficient people would agree with us that so much was worth preserving in its proper place for them to come and make its further maintenance possible. The refurbishing of the Holland wing remained for the future, although that has now been done. Apart from the bedrooms up above, there are three main rooms there, which we now show on special occasions, and they contain, I must admit selfishly, some of my favourite paintings. There are the Canalettos in our own dining-room and in the main saloon I have kept the remarkable Bedford collection of self-portraits by famous artists—among them Cuyp, Rembrandt, Hals, Jan Both, David Teniers, Jean Baptiste Colbert and Hogarth.

Out in the grounds we had also put in order the Sculpture Gallery, built as an orangery by Henry Holland. It contains the collection of marbles purchased by the fifth duke during his grand tour. Distinguished Whig politicians stand cheek by jowl with Roman patriots and there is a transplanted, and extremely handsome, early Roman mosaic floor.

Henry Holland's Chinese Dairy at the side of the north stable block was also refurbished. It was built to house a collection of porcelain and is a typical oriental folly of the period. The lake just in front of it provides anyone with a taste for it with an opportunity for making friends with its golden carp. This was a curious fancy of my father, who used to give them names based on their appearance. He developed quite a circus act with them. He had three bells mounted on the bank and when he rang the largest bell the largest fish used to rise to be fed, and so on. He used to bring them bits of bread and grain and they made hideous sucking noises as they took them out of his hand. They probably lost the trick of it when he died, and I suspect a number of them fell victims to a particularly intelligent kingfisher which used to haunt the place.

Opening day dawned with our fingers well crossed. We had no idea what to expect: half a dozen people on bicycles or a queue of cars as far as Dunstable. We had a whole party of friends and relations down to act as guides, all of them carefully primed and briefed about the history of the house in general, and the contents of the particular room to which they were assigned. We had an hilarious, if slightly nervous, early lunch and then took up our stations. Eventually someone saw two cars and a bicycle coming up the drive, and we all rushed to the windows to look at our first visitors. In fact I think the interest on that first day was if anything reversed.

Everything went with a bang from the start. All the arrangements worked out as we had planned and soon the car park was nearly full and people pouring through the house. Included among them was a good acquaintance who came up to me and said: 'I must say you give your guides a pretty easy time.' I went back with him to a room he had just passed through and found one of the house guests who had been deputed as guide snoring peacefully on a sofa, sleeping off too good a lunch. Visitors were streaming past him quite unperturbed.

Denise Ebury, my sister-in-law, who is very intelligent and made a very good guide, had worked up a really first-class lecture for her room which she repeated tirelessly and at great length. One of her old school friends was working in the next room, and one elderly lady visitor came up to her and said: 'You should tell that guide next door she ought to shut up. She talks too much.' Of course she could not wait to pass this on to Denise and things became a little monosyllabic in that corner for a time.

We had been slightly worried about the possibility of pilfering, but the first day brought the only two incidents we have ever had. One lady was caught snipping a piece out of one of the brocade curtains as a souvenir, and a little dog we had brought with us from South Africa was carried off by one of the visitors, and never seen again.

The only other untoward incident during the first week occurred when a man came up to Lydia and put sixpence in her hand as a tip, saying, 'That's for you, ducks.' My wife, who knew a piece of bread and butter when she saw it, did a grateful bob and said, 'Thank you, sir.'

Young Francis also saw possibilities of personal profit. He used to go round collecting all sorts of friends among the children who had come with their parents, and been left to amuse themselves in the playground. We found him conducting a private tour of his own, clutching a great handful of sixpences which he had charged the children for rides down the slide. Lydia was quite cross with him and told him that he had been very naughty because the playground was free. His answer set us something of a poser: 'You and Daddy take money,' he said. 'Why shouldn't I?'

CHAPTER ELEVEN

HOME AND TRY

THAT first year we had 181,000 visitors, far more than my trustees or indeed anybody else thought we could possibly attract. All the hard work had paid off. By putting ourselves out to make people feel welcome, and by providing the sort of attractions that people look for on a free day, we had jumped straight into the front rank of the stately homes business. Only the Duke of Devonshire at Chatsworth was doing better than we were, and he had years of experience and organization behind him. We were in business, and if only we could keep it up Woburn would be saved for the family.

I soon found, somewhat to my embarrassment, that one of the principal attractions of the house was myself. People seemed delighted to come up and chat and as I am an old gossip by nature we get on extremely well. I soon developed a routine of making a couple of circuit tours during the afternoon, talking and smiling away. In between I spend about three hours in the souvenir-room in the house, or the second stall we have out in the grounds, signing autographs and selling guide-books. The extraordinary thing is that sales go up by thirty or fifty per cent while I am there. Everyone wants to shake me by the hand or have my photograph taken with mum, dad and the kids. I had no idea until I started this sort of thing that one has separate muscles for smiling. At the end of the day my face aches so much that I think if I grin once more I shall go crazy. The terrible thing is that when I get back with the family and someone says something really funny the pain when I laugh is unbearable.

I have developed a habit of asking visitors what they like best. It helps with any alterations we make in the layout and enables us to know what to emphasize when we revise the guide-books. 'What do you like best in the house?' I asked a lady one day. 'Oh, I like the brass best, the lovely brass you have in your dining-room'—which is our best Bedford gold plate. Another lady who had walked past the Van Dycks, the china and all our other treasures, said that the thing she liked best was the nice linoleum we had on the floor. She wanted some for her kitchen and asked where we had got it from. My wife had the worst shock. A man came up, leaned forward very confidentially, and she thought he was going to ask some questions about the Gainsborough or the silver. 'Can you tell me where I can be very quietly sick?' he asked. She jumped back and led him quickly out.

'Have you any other postcards of the ruin?' another lady asked rather disparagingly; but the know-alls are the worst. Two ladies were making the tour one day, one a little ahead of the other. 'Is there anything there?' one of them asked her friend in the next room. 'Oh, no,' replied the other in a loud voice, 'there's nothing at all. They had a sale here before the war and Queen Mary bought it all. There's nothing of consequence left whatsoever.' Of course there had been no sale and Queen Mary had never bought a thing, but if I had told them I doubt if they would have believed me.

The only real miscalculation we made was in the provision of toilet facilities. It had not occurred to us that people who had spent three hours in a coach think first of their natural functions when they arrive, so that at one time we had longer queues for the lavatories than we did for the house, and one poor gentleman died of a heart attack when he finally got inside. We had to endure a number of complaints before the situation was righted. I was crossing over Piccadilly at the bottom of Bond Street one day, with the traffic zooming past in every direction, when the lady on the traffic island with me suddenly looked up and said: 'Are you the Duke of Bedford?' I had to acknowledge that I was. 'I want a word with you, young man,' she went on. 'I came down to Woburn with my Women's Institute and I had to queue up fifteen minutes for the toilet. It's not good enough.' She had me backed up against the traffic, so I reassured her hastily that we were building new ones, and that the next time she came she would not have to wait so long.

For some unknown reason my father had installed nine lavatories in the cellar. As neither he nor any of his guests ever drank, I cannot think what they were for. They were a little primitive, but we pressed them into temporary service while building better accommodation elsewhere. One poor husband who had been waiting at the top of the stairs for his wife for about twenty minutes, asked her what it was like. 'Oh, it's fine,' she replied crushingly. 'You walk for a mile, wait for an hour and then go into a filthy dirty place. It's fine down there!' Things, may I add hastily, are much better now.

We still get a few written complaints, most of them about unimportant things, but I take them all seriously, send a written reply and try to put matters right where necessary. One lady sent an endless list of complaints about trivia—the colour of certain chair covers in some rooms did not go with the walls, some of the magazines on the tables were not the current numbers and so on. I wrote back saying that we tried to satisfy every customer to the very best of our ability and felt quite sure that we had satisfied her, as clearly her main interest in life was grumbling.

We get every conceivable nationality. Most South Africans know we have lived in their country for a time and address me in Afrikaans. Fortunately I have about ten phrases, and as I can usually get the gist of their questions, these few words go down very well. The odd thing is that the Americans by and large are the poorest spenders of all. Most of them come to England on inclusive tours and seem to have little spare cash left over. It is the great British public which has the money. We still have a good many people who offer tips. It is all rather charming. By now most of them know perfectly well who we are, but they come up and say that they know how difficult things are, and leave a sixpence or a shilling, or tell us to keep the change if we are selling a souvenir. They are always the people who really know what a difference sixpence or a shilling can make, which I find very touching. They always want to know how long we work. My wife was asked once when her day off was, how long she had been on the staff and what it was like working there. She said she had been on the staff for some time and hoped to be there a certain time longer.

Like any other profession, it is no good resting on your laurels. Unless we think up new attractions with which to tempt people, or persuade them to come a second or third time, they will go elsewhere. Although the actual contents and layout of the house cannot be altered to any major degree, the amenities in the park are capable of infinite variety, and I have made it my business over the years since to see that there was always something new to offer in the grounds. We are in a competitive business and like any other commercial undertaking, half the battle is publicity. Unless you draw attention to yourself and your wares, people will take no notice of you.

In order to make sure that people do not forget that they are welcome at Woburn, I have thrust myself quite un-ashamedly in the public eye. I have been accused of being undignified. That is quite true, I am. If you take your dignity to a pawnbroker he won't give you much for it. My relatives think I am crazy, but I intend to keep up with the times. I don't think there is any point in being toffee-nosed or sticking your nose in the air and pretending you're something you are not. Being a showman is much more fun than sitting about in dignity or potting pheasants. In show business I have made infinitely more friends than I would ever have made trailing across a grouse moor.

A lot of visitors come in coaches, so at the end of the first year we had a party at Woburn to which we asked all the motor-coach owners and traffic managers of the big coach undertakings. We gave them tea and a free tour of the Abbey in order to pick up hints as to how we might best serve the interests of their customers, and ensure their cooperation in bringing people to us. As a result, for the second year we put up a new milk-bar in the stables, decorated in sky-blue tiles bearing a duke's coronet. People seemed to like it, and it has been very popular.

During 1957 we held scooter rallies and traction-engine rallies, installed espresso coffee machines and a juke-box in the milk-bar, which seemed to tickle the public's fancy. Hughie Green had me on his television show; I played the wash-board for a visiting skiffle group, which has made more people regard me as a human being than anything else I have ever done. As an admirer of both Arthur Miller and his wife, I invited Marilyn Monroe to spend the week-end and sleep in Queen Victoria's bed. Unfortunately she could not come.

Once you have lent yourself for publicity purposes, it is surprising how much you attract without planning it. One of the film companies had asked me to speak the commentary on a documentary film. We had to go out to Switzerland to take some location shots and, bless my soul, when we were up the Jungfrau Joch, if we did not get cut off from the main party in a fog. We had a donkey with us who at one point refused to go any further, so we stood shivering and cursing the wretched beast for a couple of hours. When the fog lifted we found that it had stopped a few feet short of a deep crevasse in which we would inevitably have fallen. Of course the story was all over the papers.

James Boyd, the butler, who will do anything if he thinks it helps me or Woburn, allowed me to put him up as a prize in an American competition to be butler for a week-end to an American family. We saw him off from London Airport and of course the publicity was tremendous, but the poor man had rather a thin time of it and came back complaining that they had expected him to watch the baby and wash nappies. The American press turned the whole thing into a circus. The winner's house was invaded by so many camera-men and newspaper reporters, recording every detail of his activities, that he was unable to carry out his normal duties at all. By the time they left the house looked as if a bomb had hit it, but it was all in a good cause.

It has got to the point now where almost anything we plan attracts attention. We have water-scooters on one of the lakes and now encourage people to try the coarse fishing. When the nudist societies complained that they could find nowhere to hold their camps, I willingly offered them a corner of Woburn park. It is large enough and well wooded; they are decent, well-behaved people and I am one of the few landowners who can offer them a little privacy. We are thinking of organizing a caravan club where people can park their caravans and I think there is probably a market for sight-seeing trips in aeroplanes, which we can easily accommodate, using the field from which my grand-mother used to take off. Now that we have the roads in the park in really good order we are going to run coach-and-four tours. Several of the old family coaches are still in the stables, and they might just as well earn their keep.

We improve the catering facilities all the time as we find that people regard a good tea as an essential component of a day out. A newspaper reported once that someone had complained that we were not giving value for money in the tea-room. I was rather cross about this as it is a point we watch very closely. I challenged the newspaper to send a reporter down as a simple visitor, try the tea we provide and give a full account of whether he thought it value for money or not. Fortunately they followed up the suggestion and his glowing report soon put a stop to that one.

Someone has even suggested that we ought to make an additional charge for seeing our ghost. There is a rather curious and tiresome ghost at Woburn which opens the door of the room where we have our television set, walks through and never bothers to shut it. Why it troubles with the door at all I cannot imagine, but the apparition is rather too spasmodic to warrant an extra fee.

Sometimes, with the best will in the world the publicity ideas go wrong. I went to a lot of trouble to organize an exhibition tour of Canada and the United States with some of the best Woburn paintings during the off-season. I thought it would attract American visitors to the Abbey and help the British tourist trade in general. Then the Treasury stepped in. They said they were pictures of national importance, and as they did not know under what conditions they would be exhibited in America, they could not permit them to be exported. Perhaps they thought I was going to flog them to some Texas oil millionaire, but I would have imagined it was something they could have kept a check on. If they cared a little more whether my roof fell in or not I would have a little more sympathy with their scruples. I refused to accept their veto as final and in the autumn of 1958 they allowed me to carry out the tour.

We are, of course, extremely lucky in the situation of Woburn. It is within easy reach of both London and the Midlands, but even so the attendance figures must prove that we offer something that people want. The second year we had 234,000 visitors, in the third the figure leapt to 372,000, and in 1958 we reached nearly half a million by opening the house on Sundays during the winter. We now attract nearly double the number of visitors to our nearest rival, Chatsworth. This must prove that we provide something unique, both as regards situation, contents and surroundings.

The maximum number of people we have had on any one day was 37,000 on Whit Monday 1958. That is a lot of people, at least the equivalent of a first division football stadium full. The curious thing is that you never get the impression of so many people around, and although the car parks give an indication they are well dispersed and easy of access. After all we have more than 3,000 acres inside the park walls and even seven people an acre is not a very great mass of people. They pay their half-crown as they enter the lodge gates and it is very odd how over the years not more than a third of them makes the tour of the actual house, although it is all included in the price. It makes no difference whether there is a queue or not. On Sundays we charge an extra shilling for entering the Abbey, chiefly in the hope of persuading people to stagger their visits and come more often on weekdays.

I am often asked whether they do not leave a terrible mess. There is always a certain amount of litter to clear up, but with the steady income we can employ people to do it. In any case if you have friends in for a drink in your house, think what a mess they often leave. So if you have thousands of people, you cannot expect them all to be tidy. There is a certain amount of wear and tear, but nothing out of the ordinary, and the visitors are terribly good with the animals, who seem to thrive on the attention and publicity as much as I do.

As soon as we found that Woburn was going to be a success, we spent less and less time in our Jersey house. I cannot say I ever found the company on the island particularly attractive, and even taxation relief could not make up for the boredom. We sold our house again in 1957 and bought in exchange a London house. I was lucky enough to obtain the freehold of the lovely old Georgian residence on the Chelsea Embankment where Whistler did most of his work. The view from the sitting-room window is exactly that depicted in his marvellous dawn picture of the Thames in morning mist. We only use it as a *pied-à-terre* when we have to attend functions in London, and find it provides a very useful ancillary source of income by letting it out for wedding receptions. Even at week-ends when we are always at Woburn to greet the main flow of visitors, we have a standing contract with a caterer for the London house to accommodate Jewish wedding parties, which is a nice piece of interdenominational juggling.

One of the most pleasant aspects of making Woburn available to the public has been the conscious change in my own attitude to the operation. I will not try and pretend that I embarked on the idea primarily out of a sense of social obligation. Certainly I wanted other people to share in the pleasure that all these lovely things we possess can afford, but the initial drive was purely economic. I knew that there was a great shortage of money, and as I love Woburn more than anything else in the world, I wanted to find some way of perpetuating it intact. Opening it to the public seemed the only way of doing it.

It was not until the operation had settled down that I really discovered the enormous amount of pleasure and satisfaction there is in giving other people happiness. At first I was after their money, and it was only later that I discovered that the best way of persuading them to part with their money was to give them a good time, to give them value for their half-crowns. Fortunately I like other people very much; I like talking to them and meeting them. I do not know how dukes are meant to behave, but apparently I do not conform to what people expect. I chat away and it seems to go down very well, I do not know why. People seem to like it, at least the people who come to look at the house do. I suspect some of my fellow peers disapprove of my behaviour and approach, but frankly I couldn't care less. Perhaps a little more friendliness on their part would make them more popular and more successful.

It may well be that I have had a better background training than they have, or than my father and grandfather had, to deal with ordinary people. When I was a journalist I had to be nice to people in order to get my story, and when I was very hard up before the war I had to make myself agreeable in order to be invited to dinner or a dance. I find it a very true axiom in life that what you get out of it depends directly on how much you put into it. It is much easier to be agreeable to people than to be upstage, and the response is out of all proportion to the effort.

We run our own wing of Woburn on a very modest scale. Where my grandfather had scores of servants in Belgrave Square and at the Abbey, we make do with seven, to cover both houses, with all the public engagements that the stately-home business entails. We do have fourteen dailies and six night-watchmen who come in on a part-time basis from Woburn village, but their job is to clean and look after the whole vast complex of the house, including the public rooms and the tea-room and restaurant in the stables. We keep no part of the park for ourselves. There are a few notices up marking off sections of it as a private area, but this is chiefly for the protection of the animals, and we expect no further rights in the grounds than we give our visitors. We are perfectly happy to share the pleasures of the estate with them.

Although we are always on hand during the visiting season, which is April to September, we have to work even harder during the winter. It is what you organize during the off-season that brings in the people during the summer. The American travel agencies want all their advance information by the autumn of the previous year, and the British coach companies, Women's Institutes, townswomen's guilds and clubs all want to know the new programme in advance by December or January. I go round the country lecturing, speaking to different societies and trying to interest people who are likely to bring parties during the visiting months. Future plans include a motel, licensed premises and a beer garden, and, if necessary, a fun fair.

Although we had a gross income from Woburn of some eighty thousand pounds in 1958, it should not be supposed that this shows a penny of profit. The place tumbles down much more quickly than you can possibly keep it going. The central heating alone costs five thousand pounds a year, sixteen thousand pounds have just gone on re-roofing the stables, and we have spent more than forty thousand pounds on keeping the fabric of the outside walls intact. The staff, the guides, the attendants, the litter-clearers, the car-park attendants, all have to be paid, and everyone knows the levels wages have reached in these days. The best that can be said is that we are nearly breaking even, and that for the moment, at any rate, there is no danger of Woburn falling down from sheer neglect. It does not help with the death duties at all, it just means that Woburn can be kept going without providing too great a strain on the remaining estate.

The future is by no means certain. I have a serious difference of opinion with the family trustees, who consider that the Abbey should be handed over to the National Trust, which is one way of helping to pay death duties, although that means that it passes irrevocably out of the family and even under the most favourable arrangement would reduce me and my son and our successors to the status of tenants in our own house. Once that happens, then your roots have gone, and if a place like Woburn means anything in terms of history and tradition, then it is only because of the personal identification with it of the family that has built it up. The trustees want to hold on to the remains of the Bloomsbury estate as the financial backbone of the trust they are under an obligation to maintain, and hive off almost everything else.

It is an extraordinary situation. I have no legal rights in the matter at all. I am not even a member of the trust and cannot influence its composition. Its members are self-perpetuating and they can co-opt whomsoever they see fit. I have absolutely no authority whatsoever. This may sound incredible, but it is all a result of the provisions my grandfather and father made when I was sixteen. All I have is the family title. I live at Woburn by the grace of the trustees. Most of them are of my father's generation and find it difficult to appreciate my point of view. At least they are more reasonable to deal with than my father and grandfather were. They recognize that I have a certain position in the matter and that I am entitled to a certain income as head of the family. I am dependent on them for every penny. If I want a new bath or toilet facilities put in at Woburn, or three new public lavatories for the use of our stream of visitors, I have to go and ask the trustees if the work may be done. Any capital expenditure, even of the most trivial sort, has to be authorized by them.

The original trust, which my father and grandfather modified, was a tricky enough document anyway. It was originally formulated by the sixth duke, and legally any one of his descendants can inherit the property at the discretion of the trustees. As he had thirteen children, there must be a couple of hundred vague cousins around who could qualify. When my son inherits, I am fiercely determined that whatever comes to him shall include the Abbey. I do not know of any great family that has survived the loss of its house, and if I succeed in passing it on to him, I shall have done that part of my duty.

I do have the utmost difficulty in persuading the trustees of the potentiality of Woburn to contribute to the upkeep of the estate. While recognizing that I have created something out of nothing in four years, they still tend to regard it as a temporary success, and pin their faith in Victorian ideas of property-owning with fixed substantial rents as the only proper economic basis. I feel that there is a much bigger future in the kind of happy Hampstead atmosphere at Woburn than there is for the bloated landlord holding on to his property and robbing the poor tenant, which is sure to be the attitude of some Socialist government if they get back into power. If they receive a mandate to municipalize or nationalize landed property then there will be nothing I can do about it, and however much Bloomsbury may bring in now it will cease being a source of income from that moment.

We are still in the process of trying to find the last three million pounds in death duties. It is almost impossible to specify the exact figure, as the valuers on both sides are engaged in endless argument about the worth of each piece of property as it comes up for consideration, and no final figure can be set until it is actually sold. The Chenies estate was sold soon after my father died. What is left of the Tudor mansion that belonged to the first Earl of Bedford is now a farmhouse. Part of the Tavistock estate has already gone, but the status of the remainder is in suspense. Part of the Bloomsbury estate itself was sold in 1958 and we earned a million pounds for the Treasury from three large blocks adjacent to New Oxford Street, High Holborn and Southampton Row. My father left something like eight hundred thousand pounds in stocks and shares, cash and other immediately realizable securities. This was nearly all left outside the family and was not available to pay the duty on the settled estate. I only wish the Treasury would take at their face value the crateful of Russian bonds that my grandfather bought before the First World War with the proceeds of Covent Garden and Long Acre.

Woburn is quite a problem—it is not only the park, but about another 18,000 acres in the surrounding countryside which is let off for the greater part to working tenant farmers. Like all agricultural land, this is not a big income producer and not a particularly attractive prospect to anyone thinking of taking it off our hands, either in part or in whole. There are several hundred tied cottages on the estate, on which the controlled rent, if you please, is about one and tenpence a week. This was something introduced at the beginning of the century by my grandfather, who imposed a nominal rent so that the farm workers would not feel that they were being subjected to a form of charity. Under the Rent Restriction Act I think we can put them up about fourpence a week, but as the whole year's rent would not be enough to pay for having the doors and window-frames painted at present-day rates, it is proving impossible to keep them up. Whoever bought them would be in exactly the same position, with exactly the same statutory obligations. If a Socialist government starts commandeering houses they are welcome to this little lot with pleasure.

The art treasures and furniture at Woburn are, I suppose, at a very rough estimate, worth about another million and a half pounds. While some of these could be handed over to the Treasury at their estimated value in settlement of estate duty, as has been done at Chatsworth, look at the outcry that would be caused among people who prefer to see these things in their natural surroundings. Almost all the paintings and *objets d'art* at Woburn have a direct family connexion and would lose much of their atmosphere if displayed along with rows of others in some impersonal museum.

I suppose if we could find about three hundred thousand pounds to endow Woburn and hand it over to the National Trust, they might conceivably be retained *in situ*, but then, as I have said, it would no longer be the family's home, and I do not think that any of us would feel like lavishing the care on it that we have expended over the last few years, and which alone makes it a living thing. The position at the time of writing is that the agreement of the National Trust to take over the property is in abeyance. I have made it clear that I would be a very unwilling tenant, so for the time being they have withdrawn their offer. Needless to say, my trustees are not exactly pleased.

I have no particular case of conscience about taking rents from the Bloomsbury estate. There are hundreds of thousands of people in Britain living on the income from property and as long as this is regarded as a legal way of investing money I do not see why I should be expected to regard it as immoral. Most of our tenants in Bloomsbury now are business concerns, either commercial firms, publishers, London University, or something of the sort. Our estate office has always granted very reasonable leases, and people are very much better off with us than they are with some of the real sharks who infest the property market. But both for sentimental and business reasons I regard the running of Woburn on its present basis as a much better long-term proposition than keeping our fingers crossed and hanging on blindly to Bloomsbury.

In due course my son will have to face up to this problem in his turn. I only hope we have given him and his brothers a better preparation for life and its responsibilities than I ever had. Lydia has been a wonderful mother to them all. We have never made any sort of differentiation between one family and the other, and they all regard us as their father and mother. We are an extremely happy family and there is a wonderful feeling of security and peace. Remembering my own short commons and the constant interference of my father with every phase of my existence, I may have gone to the other extreme. I probably give them too much money, but I leave them more or less to work out their own plan of living and only intervene with such guidance as I am able to give on very rare occasions. They were at day-school and boarding-school in South Africa, and when we came back to England we found that the standard was very different.

They were all about eighteen months behindhand so it meant a lot of hard work for them to catch up. I sent Robin, the Marquess of Tavistock, to school in Switzerland, where I hoped he would pick up French, but all he learnt to speak was American, because many of the boys came from the States and spoke neither French nor the Queen's English. He developed such a passion for America that I sent him off to high-school there to see if that would cure him, but now he has passed his exam into Harvard it looks as if he will be there for some time. Lorna, my wife's daughter, has already come out. In fact, the dance we had for her at Woburn in the summer of 1957 was the first to be held at the Abbey for nearly a hundred years. Gavin, the son of the Lyle marriage, is at Eton.

I was a little worried about Rudolf, my second boy, for a while. The eldest three were eighteen, seventeen and sixteen, when he was fourteen and so, inevitably, he was always odd man out. There was a time when I felt he was growing up rather like I was at his age, very introverted. You could never get near to him, or know what he was thinking or feeling. Then I sent him to Gordonstoun, where he is very happy, and it has done wonders for him. It has had a marvellous effect on his whole character and it is a very remarkable school. They concentrate much more on developing people's self-respect and character, before they get on with the academic side of it, and I am sure this is the right way of setting about things.

I would like to send our youngest, Francis, there in due course. I think he is going to be the clever one of the family. We used to watch like hawks over the health of the four eldest, trying to make sure they got masses of food and exercise. As a result they have all turned out skinny, thin children, but we let the baby run riot. He drinks red wine and eats Gruyère cheese and lobster and then probably eats nothing for two or three days, existing on endless bottles of Coca-Cola. He is infinitely fitter and more lively than the others ever were and as clever as a monkey.

About the only recent family tradition to which I have

been faithful is my non-involvement in politics. Our fortune was made by the services the Bedfords rendered in the sixteenth and seventeenth centuries, and the fourth and fifth dukes played a very prominent part in the history of the eighteenth century, but for the last hundred and fifty years we have taken a back seat. This is not the day and age to revive the earlier pattern merely because as a duke I am a member of the House of Lords. I can see very little justification for the hereditary peer in politics, as by and large they have ceased to be representative of the governing class any more.

I am very much in favour of the reform of the House of Lords and the bringing in of life peers. I think a second chamber is a desirable component of the machinery of government. If there is a real chance of it being reconstituted in a different form I would be very interested to take part in its debates, but I do not feel that birth alone is a sufficient justification to go and blow your top on things to do with government. If any of us with hereditary titles has become prominent in other connexions, and is able to represent and talk knowledgeably about matters which lie in the interest of substantial sections of the population, then I think we probably have a modest part to play. If we are ever invited to state our intention irrevocably, one way or the other, of attending the House of Lords, I would certainly answer in the affirmative, as I feel there are one or two matters which affect the economic life of this country, particularly the tourist trade, on which I can start to talk as an expert.

I have attended a number of debates but I have yet to make my maiden speech. You have to know so much about the rules and procedure of the House and I am terrified of making a fool of myself when I stand up. My father has left such an unhappy memory of his contributions that I would hate to do anything which annoyed or embarrassed my fellow peers, although, heaven knows, I have little enough contact with them. Nominally I attend as a Conservative, but I do not think I have exchanged more than the time of day with the Marquess of Salisbury, the party leader in the Lords.

I have very little time for the game of politics as such. Most politicians seem to enter the profession because they like the sound of their own voices, and because they are ambitious for themselves. I often wonder how really interested they are in the good of the people they govern; they seem far more interested to me in power itself. Far too few people in the Commons behave as individuals of independent mind. Half the Conservatives are in because they have succeeded in making the largest donation to the local constituency association, and half the Labour people are there by nomination of their trade unions. They are lobbyists rather than Members of Parliament and none of them seems to have any freedom of action at all.

Opening Woburn to the public is involving me more and more in the ramifications of the tourist trade as a whole. I have learnt one important lesson, that if you offer people value for money they will come and spend it. I only wish the British tourist industry had learnt the same lesson. We could double the dollar and foreign currency income of this country if we offered better facilities, improved the standards of our hotels and spent as much on advertising as our other main rivals in Europe. The only places Americans have ever heard of outside London are Oxford, Cambridge, Stratford and Edinburgh. The British Holiday Travel Association does its best, in fact I am even a member of it myself, but it gets such a miserly and minuscule budget from the Board of Trade that it cannot hope to do the job properly.

We have to listen to all these exhortations from the government to increase the export trade, yet they will not lift a finger to give practical help to what could be far and away the largest single item of foreign income of all, earned right here at home, and providing tangible employment and cash for scores of thousands of people. I would have thought that with loans and mortgages any number of the large country houses dotted around the countryside, probably falling down because the owners cannot afford the upkeep, could be converted into paying hotels and holiday centres for tourists. Several European countries have a government department whose sole business is to foster the tourist trade, and we shall never succeed in competing with them until we follow suit.

Of course the government cannot do everything. The different regions of England and individual hotel-keepers are not only going to have to sell themselves much more attractively, but the standards of catering and accommodation will have to be improved immensely. There is still too much blotting-paper and bill-poster's paste on the menu and too many toilet and bathroom facilities belong to an age the Americans left behind two generations ago. Above all, we need a change in attitude.

Service with a smile no longer seems to form part of the British way of life. We like to think we have a reputation for good manners, but my experience is that service is too often grudging, perfunctory and bad-tempered. Hotels insist on serving meals at impossible hours, and although some modifications in the Wages and Catering Act are probably necessary, this will still not alter the attitude of the people who benefit by it unless they come to regard their work as a matter of pride. Petrol stations close down just as you need that last evening refill, provincial railway stations are enough to drive most people to take the next 'plane out of the country, and there is far too much of a 'take it or leave it' atmosphere, which the British seem to tolerate, but which enrages tourists.

I have by now acquired quite a lot of practical experience in the business of catering for and entertaining large numbers of people. I know the mechanics of transporting them and meeting their wishes, and can lay reasonable claim to having developed promotion and advertising campaigns to attract them. Our lovely old country houses in England offer something unique and tell of our tradition and heritage in a manner hardly matched by any other medium. Consider the success of the French in promoting the chain of châteaux on the Loire. Yet we have ten times as many beautiful buildings to show, each of them a living entity and not just a hollow shell. If anybody thinks my advice and experience in this connexion is useful, I would be happy to give it, either in an official or a personal capacity.

Here then is a pattern for present activity and future endeavour. I suppose I could make life very much easier for myself if I abandoned all the worries of Woburn, accepted such part of the family income as the trustees saw fit to channel my way, and joined some of my kind lolling in the sun in the Bahamas. I would be bored silly and not feel I was doing my job. The wheel has come full circle with a vengeance. I find myself trying to perpetuate the heritage of the family, to which I did not even know I belonged until I was in my teens, and accepting responsibilities which my grandfather and father were careful to prevent my assuming until I was in my late thirties. No one can say life does not have its curious quirks.

At Woburn now, we are converting the bedroom floor of the Holland wing into a series of self-contained flatlets. If we can keep the house, then every member of the family will have a home, even if we have to do without servants altogether.

I may be the thirteenth duke, but if we can keep Woburn Abbey I shall count myself a very lucky man.

INDEX

215

217

219